YOUR CAPTAIN'S TREASURE

LACEY BUCKLES

Lacey Buckles
xox

This is a work of fiction. Names, characters, places, and incidents either are the product of the author's imagination or are used fictitiously. Any resemblance to actual persons, living or dead, events, or locales is entirely coincidental.

1

ISBN 978-1-913673-20-8

CONTENT WARNING

This story includes:

- Threat of rape/sexual violence (not enacted)
- Public sex
- Forced nudity
- Power imbalance and hints of a master/servant dynamic

While dark themes are present, the sexual relationship between the protagonists is ultimately consensual, emotionally layered, and rooted in mutual desire. Readers who enjoy complex power dynamics with a deeply protective dominant partner will find a rich, rewarding experience here.

The Bookbinder's Invitation

Ah...

So you found me.

How curious. How promising.

Not everyone hears the call. Not everyone dares to open a book like this. But *you*... you've always wanted more, haven't you? More danger. More pleasure. More dark, decadent surrender.

Good. You'll find it here.

These stories were not written—they were *felt.* Fed by longing. Shaped by shadows. Bound in ink, blood, and desire. And I? I am their keeper. Their curator. Their collector. You may call me the Bookbinder.

Come closer. Read slowly. Let each story take root in you.

I promise, I'm always watching. And when the time is right...

...I'll have a story of my own to tell.

As for this story...

Well, salt on the skin. Fire in the blood. And the kind of danger that smells like rum, sweat, and surrender.

Hester thinks she's clever. She's survived worse than pirate ships and filthy glares. But Captain Blackthorne is not like other men. He doesn't take what he wants—he makes you give it to him.

Willingly. Breathlessly. And with just a hint of shame.

This tale is bound in rope and riddles, bruised lips and dark devotion. A treasure worth taking. A captain worth obeying.

If you've come from the collection, you may pick up the story again at Chapter Five (the deep end). Otherwise, let the story unfold from the very first page.

The waves are rising, darling reader. I wonder… will you be strong enough to stay afloat? Or will you become—
Your Captain's Treasure.

CHAPTER ONE

The tavern is a cacophony of noise—raucous laughter, shouted orders, and the ever-present clinking of tankards. The scent of spilled ale and salt air mingles in the heavy warmth of the room, thick with the sweat of sailors fresh off their ships. I weave through the crowd, a tray of full tankards balanced against my hip, dodging grasping hands and sidestepping leering grins with the ease of long practice. My shoulders ache from carrying tray after tray, and my calves burn from darting between tables, but there's no time to rest.

"Come on, love, give us a smile!" A ruddy-faced sailor bellows, his grin wide and toothless as he leans far too close. The smell of stale rum clings to him, and I step back just out of his reach.

"You'll get a smile when you've paid your tab, Jonah," I say with a wink, sliding his tankard onto the table and moving on before he can reply.

I can feel eyes on me everywhere I go—assessing, weighing, and hoping for a chance to get their hands on something they shouldn't. My bodice does little to protect me, my assets on full display as required by the tavern's owner. More cleavage means more coin, or so he says. It's a game I've grown tired of, but a game I know how to play well.

"Hester!" The barman's voice cuts through the noise like a whip crack, and I wince. I glance toward the bar where Old Al stands, his face flushed red, a scowl deepening the lines around his mouth. "That table in the corner's been waitin' too long! What're ye doin', takin' a holiday?"

I grit my teeth, adjusting the tray on my hip. "I'm run off my feet, Al. Ask one of the lads to—"

"Lads ain't what the customers want," he interrupts, wiping down the bar with a filthy rag. "Get to it, girl, or you'll find yourself out in the street!"

Biting back my retort, I push through the crowd, muttering curses under my breath. My back aches, my feet throb, and sweat sticks my hair to the nape of my neck, but the work doesn't stop. I dodge a stumbling drunk, narrowly avoiding an elbow to my ribs, and press on.

"Oi, sweetheart!" A loud voice cuts through the din, and I turn to see a man at the corner table spinning a gold coin between his fingers. He's different from the others—not just in the way he dresses, with a finer coat and a tricorn hat that hasn't seen too many storms, but in the way he watches me. Sharper. Calculating.

"Have a seat, will ye?" he says, patting the empty chair beside him. "Just a moment o' your time, I promise."

I hesitate, glancing at the crowded room, but curiosity wins out. With a weary sigh, I slide into the seat, the wooden chair creaking beneath me.

"What's your game, then?" I ask, crossing my arms, my patience worn thin by a long evening of fending off drunken advances.

He grins, flashing a gold tooth among the crooked, stained

once. “No game, love. I’ve an offer for you.” He spins the coin again, the gold catching the dim light. “Thomas Briggs, first mate of The Stormchaser, at your service.” He lifts his hat slightly as he introduces himself. He looks as if he expects me to be impressed, but I’ve met more men claiming to be first mates than I can count. “I’ll give you one coin for every man aboard our ship, if you come along and keep us in good company.”

I arch a brow, unimpressed. “You want me to sail with a ship full of men and... what? Pour their drinks at sea?” My voice drips with scepticism.

“Aye,” he says smoothly. “And keep their spirits high, if ye catch my meaning.”

I let out a soft laugh, shaking my head. “I’ve no desire to be tossed about on the waves by the likes of you and your crew. I’ll pass.”

“Think it over, love. There’s more gold where that came from.” He flicks the coin across the table, and I snatch it up before it rolls off the edge. I weigh it in my hand for a moment before slipping it into my apron. That one guinea is more than I make in three months. It’s no ordinary tip. It’s a promise.

“I’ll think on it,” I say, rising to my feet and returning to my rounds.

The evening drags on, my feet aching and my patience worn thin. Another sailor pulls me onto his lap, and it takes all my strength not to slap him outright. A moment later, another drunkard sways on his feet and vomits right at my feet, the acrid stench curling up into my nostrils. I wrinkle my nose and sigh, stepping back and muttering a curse under my breath.

As I mop up the mess, the first mate’s voice comes from behind me. “Changed your mind yet, love?”

I glance over my shoulder, eyeing him as he leans casually against the bar. The room stinks of sweat and spilled beer, and I suddenly feel as though I'll drown in it if I stay another night.

"How many men?" I ask over the hubbub around us.

"I've a crew of seventy men."

I wipe my hands on my apron and stare down at the mop. My chest tightens, my mind racing through the risks. Leaving everything behind, sailing with men I don't know—men who may not have my best interests at heart. But then I think of the gold, of the way my life could change with seventy gold coins in my purse. A fresh start. A chance to be something more than a tavern wench scraping by on crumbs.

I take a deep breath, my fingers curling into fists. There's no choice, not really. "Aye. I'm in."

He grins, tipping his hat. "Smart girl. We set sail at dawn."

The docks are alive with pre-dawn activity, a chaotic blend of shouts, creaking ropes, and the rhythmic slap of waves against the hulls of dozens of ships. I clutch a scrap of paper in my hand, the name *The Stormchaser* scrawled in a rough, untidy hand. A heavy bag hangs from my shoulder, packed with my meagre belongings, its weight digging into my aching muscles. The scents of salt, fish, and tar fill my nose, and I step carefully to avoid the slick patches where fishermen have gutted their catch from the night's haul.

As I make my way through the crowded docks, my heart pounds. Barrels and crates are being loaded onto ships, sailors barking orders and cursing at sluggish deckhands. Lanterns swing from posts, their light barely holding back the darkness that still clings to the morning. I squint at the names painted on the ships' hulls, scanning each vessel with a sinking feeling of uncertainty. Finally, I spot it—The Stormchaser.

There, at the top of the gangplank, stands the first mate—Thomas Briggs. "Hester! You came," he calls out, his voice cutting through the dockside din.

I nod and step forward, my stomach tight with nerves. "Aye, I did."

"Well, don't just stand there," he says, beckoning me up the plank. "Welcome aboard The Stormchaser. We sail with the tide."

I swallow hard and step onto the creaking wood, the salty breeze tugging at my skirts as I make my way up. The deck is a flurry of activity—men hauling ropes, stacking barrels, and shouting orders. The smell of tar and damp wood mixes with the briny sea air, and the rhythmic creak of the ship's hull beneath my feet sends a shiver up my spine.

Thomas watches me with an amused smirk, arms crossed over his chest. "You'll find the crew a lively bunch, but they know their place. Mostly," he adds with a wink. "I'll show you to your quarters, such as they are."

I nod, adjusting the strap of my heavy bag, my fingers tingle and my feet ache with the unfamiliar sensation of the ship beneath me. As I follow him below deck, the dim lantern light flickers against the wooden walls, the air thick with the scent of sea salt and unwashed bodies. My heart pounds as I step into the cramped space that will serve as my quarters—a small bunk wedged between crates of supplies, the thin mattress looking far from inviting. The corridor leading straight past it seems to be the main route from the deck to the galley, judging by the smells wafting along it. A patched curtain hangs in front of the bunk.

Thomas leans against the wall of the corridor, watching me with a bemused expression. "It's not the tavern, but it's better than what most the men get. You've got a curtain. You'll get your sea legs soon enough."

I drop my bag onto the bunk and square my shoulders. "I

suppose I will." The weight of my decision settles heavy in my chest, heavier even than the bag filled with what little I own. Seventy gold coins—enough to change my life, to buy my way into something better than serving drunken fools night after night. But the thought of leaving behind everyone I know, the only life I've ever known, gnaws at me. I don't trust these men. I don't trust this ship. But trust never put food on my table or a roof over my head. I have no choice.

"Come on," Thomas barks, and I force myself to follow him back onto the deck. "Let's take a quick turn, get you familiar with the ship," he says, leading me across the bustling deck. "That's the bow," he points ahead. "Stern's behind us. Don't get 'em mixed up, or you'll have the lads laughin' at you." I nod, taking it in as he continues. "This here's the mainmast—tallest one aboard —and those are the rigging lines, keep 'em in mind, you might need to climb 'em someday."

I glance up at the towering sails above, feeling a knot of apprehension in my chest. "Climb?"

He grins, clapping me on the back. "Aye, don't worry, we'll keep you on deck for now. Come on, I'll show you the galley and where you'll be spending most of your time." He leads me back below and past my bunk, down another narrow passage, the wooden floorboards creaking underfoot. The scent of stale bread and salted meat grows stronger as we approach a low doorway. "This here's the galley," he says, pushing it open to reveal a cramped space dominated by a large iron stove, its surface blackened with soot. A burly man in a stained apron stirs a bubbling pot, sparing me only a brief glance before returning to his work. "That's Cook. Don't cross him unless you fancy hard tack for every meal."

I step inside hesitantly, taking in the shelves lined with sacks of flour, dried fish, and rows of tin plates stacked precariously. The air is thick with the mingling scents of porridge and sweat, and my stomach twists at the thought of working in such a confined space.

Thomas gestures to an open hatch in the wall. "You'll be serving meals here, helping Cook when he needs an extra set of hands. It ain't glamorous, but it's better than scrubbing the decks."

I peer through the hatch into a larger room filled with long benches. Several men are gathered in there, trading slips of paper and various sundries they undoubtedly acquired while they were docked.

The more Thomas talks, the more I realise there will be no privacy on board, and discomfort writhes around my insides. There's nowhere to hide here, no dark corner to retreat to like back at the tavern.

"Any questions?" he asks. My mind is blank.

"No, but if I think of any later I'll ask."

He lets out a throaty bark of laughter. "I don't imagine you'll get to do much talking, lass."

He strides away and I scurry after him, wanting to ask what he means but I have a nagging feeling I already know.

He leads me back on deck. The men are preparing to set sail, pulling up the gangplank and quickly finishing securing the crates piled on deck.

"That there is the captain's quarters," he says jerking his thumb towards a door set into the raised stern of the ship. "You won't be allowed in there."

I glance at the door, chewing my lip. "What's he like? The captain?" Thomas smirks, leaning on the railing.

"Captain James Blackthorne. He's a hard man, but fair. Been sailing these waters longer than you've been alive. Knows every trick the sea's got up her sleeve, and then some. Just stay on his good side, and you'll do fine."

I wonder where this Captain Blackthorne is. I'd have liked to meet him before agreeing to work aboard his ship. But there's no time to dwell on it, as the ship suddenly lurches beneath me. The crew leaps into action, shouting commands and hauling on ropes. Sails unfurl with a snap, catching the brisk morning breeze, and the schooner begins to drift away from the dock. The rhythmic creak of the ship's timbers and the snap of canvas fill the air, accompanied by the briny scent of the open sea.

Thomas nudges me with his elbow. "You'll want to hold onto something, love. She moves quick once she's free of land."

I grip the nearest railing, my knuckles white, as the ship picks up speed. The dock recedes into the morning mist, and with it, everything I've ever known. My heart hammers in my chest, uncertainty gnawing at the edges of my resolve. But there's no turning back now.

CHAPTER TWO

The Stormchaser surges forward, slicing through the waves with a relentless urgency. The sails billow above, snapping in the wind as the crew scurries across the deck, securing ropes and shouting to one another over the crash of the sea. The salty spray kisses my cheeks, and I grip the rail tightly, watching the shoreline fade into the mist.

My stomach churns—not from the motion of the ship, but from the uncertainty gnawing at me. This isn't like any merchant vessel I've ever seen. The men are rougher, their laughter darker, and the glint in their eyes when they glance my way makes my skin crawl. The way they handle their weapons—knives tucked into belts, pistols casually holstered—tells me more than I want to know.

Thomas strides past me, sparing me a glance. "Quit gawkin', love. Time to work. Breakfast ain't gonna serve itself."

I follow him down the narrow steps into the galley. The heat hits me first, thick and suffocating, the scent of salted pork and bread hanging in the air. The galley is cramped, packed with barrels and crates that rattle with every tilt of the ship. Cook, a burly man with a permanent scowl and arms as thick as tree trunks, stands over a bubbling pot, stirring with a wooden spoon that looks more like a club.

"About time," he grunts without looking up. "Grab those plates and start servin'. These lads get cranky when they ain't fed."

I gather the tin plates, stacking them precariously on my arm. One by one, I ladle out thick porridge, the consistency reminding me more of a paste than anything fit for eating. The line of sailors waiting stretches out the door, each one grumbling, cracking crude jokes, or giving me an appraising look that makes me wish I were anywhere else.

"Hurry it up, girl!" One of them barks, slamming his empty plate down in front of me.

I force a smile, swallowing my nerves, and ladle another portion onto his plate. My arms ache under the weight, sweat beading at my brow as the ship rocks beneath my feet. The clatter of cutlery and the low rumble of conversation fill the air, but I hear snippets of talk that set my pulse racing.

"Cap'n says we're headed for the trade route—easy pickin's this time o' year."

"Hope we find another fat merchant ship soon with a good haul. The last one barely filled our pockets."

I freeze mid-scoop, my heart hammering. Trade routes? Hauls? My gaze flickers to the men surrounding me, their weathered faces etched with experience—and something far more dangerous. My hands tremble slightly as I continue serving, the realization settling heavily in my chest.

This isn't a merchant ship. This is a *pirate* ship.

A cold sweat prickles at the back of my neck. I glance toward the doorway, but Thomas is standing there, arms crossed, watching me. There's no easy escape. No turning back. I swallow hard and keep my head down, focusing on the task at hand, but the truth is clear.

I'm trapped aboard a pirate ship, and I'll have to be clever if

I want to survive.

By the time the sun sinks below the horizon, painting the sky in hues of crimson and gold, my arms ache from hauling trays and scrubbing dishes, and my feet throb from the constant motion of the ship beneath me. Cook hasn't softened, barking orders and swatting at my hands when I move too slow, but at least I've avoided drawing too much attention. I've managed to make it through my first day.

Still no sign of the captain. I've heard his name whispered—Captain Blackthorne—but he remains a ghost, his presence looming even in absence.

As darkness falls, the ship takes on a different kind of energy. The men gather on deck, their laughter turning louder, their words slurred with drink. Rum flows freely, and the scent of salt and sweat thickens in the humid night air. Lanterns swing overhead, casting flickering shadows across their rough faces. A few sailors pull out flutes and drums, striking up a lively, rollicking tune that weaves through the air, adding to the chaotic revelry. The rhythmic beat of the drums pulses through the deck, mingling with the sound of clapping hands and drunken singing. More than a few eyes linger on me longer than I'd like, and I stick close to the door under the forecastle, heart pounding.

Thomas passes by, eyeing me with a smirk. "Why don't you give 'em a twirl, love? A bit of dancing might keep 'em in line."

I hesitate, my feet frozen to the deck, but before I can slip away, a voice cuts through the raucous din. "You shouldn't be hiding in there all night, you know." I turn to find a younger sailor standing beside me, his easy smile and warm brown eyes a stark contrast to the others. His hair is tousled from the sea breeze, and there's a boyish charm about him that makes my pulse slow just a little.

"Come on," he coaxes, holding out a hand. "It's just a bit of fun. The music's good, and no one's gonna bite."

I chew my lip, glancing at the growing crowd. The thought of being swallowed by them terrifies me, but the gentle encouragement in his voice makes me falter. With a deep breath, I place my hand in his, letting him lead me onto the deck. The noise outside grows wilder—boisterous singing, the crash of tankards against wood, and the occasional scuffle breaking out. The thought of stepping out there, twirling for their amusement, knots my stomach, but the young man leading me by the hand seems nice enough.

"I'm Ben," he says over his shoulder. He fills two tankards from a barrel of beer and passes one to me. "What's your name?" He smiles, dimples showing in his cheeks. I return it with a smile of my own.

"Hester."

"Ever been on board a ship like this before?" he asks, taking a gulp of beer.

I shake my head and take a drink. The beer is dark and bitter, with a strong malty flavour that lingers on my tongue. It's warm, no doubt having sat in the barrel for too long, but there's something oddly comforting about it. The taste of salt hangs in the air, mingling with the sharp tang of the brew, making it feel like a drink born of the sea itself.

As the music swells around us, I find myself tapping my foot to the beat, the rhythm infectious despite my apprehension.

Ben grins, nudging me lightly with his elbow. "See? Told you it ain't so bad." With a laugh, he spins me in a playful twirl, and for a moment, I let myself enjoy it.

The crew cheers, their rowdy voices encouraging me to let loose. I sway to the music, my skirts swishing around my legs as I find myself moving in time with the lively tune. The warmth of the beer settles in my belly, and I throw a glance at Ben, who watches me with an approving smile. The nervous tension that had gripped me all day begins to fade, replaced with a cautious exhilaration.

Before I can catch my breath, another sailor steps in with a toothy grin, nudging Ben aside and taking my hand. “My turn, lass!” he declares, spinning me with surprising grace. Laughter bubbles up in my throat as I’m passed along to yet another partner, their calloused hands firm but not unkind. One by one, they take turns dancing me around the deck, their boisterous energy sweeping me up in the revelry.

The music quickens, feet stomping in rhythm against the wooden planks, and for a moment, I forget where I am. I forget the danger, the uncertainty. I let myself be carried away by the moment, twirling and laughing until my head spins and my cheeks flush with warmth.

I catch sight of Ben again, clapping and cheering. I’m passed around what feels like the whole crew until I come to a juddering halt in the arms of Thomas. He leers at me with his gold-toothed-smile.

“Time to really earn your coin, lass.” He shoves me into the waiting hands of a member of his crew who grips my upper arms, pinching tightly. Thomas ties thick, coarse rope around my wrists with the practised hands of someone who knows every knot. I struggle but dizziness and confusion stop me from forming any real resistance. With a nod of Thomas’s head to someone behind me, the rope around my wrists jerks my hands upward. I look up to see that the rope disappears into the darkness above. It pulls taut and my arms stretch up above my head, pulling me up onto the balls of my feet.

Panic swells in my chest and I look quickly from one face to the next, searching for an ally, someone who won’t allow this to happen to me. But every face is greedy and drunk, leering at me with hungry expectation.

Rough hands rip my dress from my body and it disappears under the feet of the closing-in sailors. Ben appears before me, his sweet charm gone and replaced with harsh movements and dark eyes. He tears my bodice and tosses it aside, then rips my undergarments off me.

"Please don't do this," I beg, tears streaming down my face.

"I call first dibs!" Ben shouts and the men around us cheer. He pinches my chin between his thumb and forefinger, scrunching my lips into a pout. He smashes his mouth against mine, probing with his rough tongue. I cry against him, trying to push him away but I sway uselessly on the spot. His hands grab at my breasts and someone else's hands grab me from behind. Ben hoists my left leg up and thrusts his hand between my thighs, grabbing callously for his intended target. I manage to jerk my head away from him and spit in his face.

He blanches, backing away from me slightly but still holding me tight. He swipes the spittle off his cheek and then breaks into a mirthless laugh.

"Turns out she's more feisty than we thought!" The men around us jeer and laugh. "Do what you like. Scratch, kick, scream. No one will hear you out here. We're going to take turns with you, use you all up again and again until you beg us to throw you to the sharks. Got it?"

Hot tears sting my eyes and my whole face collapses in vocal sobs. How could I be so foolish? How could I put myself in this situation. I'd known really what Thomas was suggesting. Why did I fool myself into believing it was anything other than this?

Ben roughly hoists me up and pokes at me again with his fingers. I try to scream but a hand clamps across my mouth from behind. I know there's no use fighting this. It's better to imagine

I'm far away and let them do what they like to the empty shell of my body. I go limp, close my eyes and try to take myself to a beach under the hot Carolina sun.

The sound of a belt buckle being undone clinks. The rustle of fabric falling. The thud of something heavy hits the deck. Ben yanks on my thighs and his manhood presses against me.

"What the devil is this?!" A voice bellows over the roar of the men. Deafening silence falls and I'm dropped unceremoniously. My toes hit the deck and my arms jerk under my own weight. My eyes open a crack, blurred with tears. Ben is hurriedly dressing himself and backing away from me. The circle widens, men backing away with shame on their brutal faces. Heavy footfalls echo in the still air.

"I asked a damn question!" The man roars. I try to focus on the newcomer, blinking away my tears.

No one offers a reply.

"Briggs." The voice barks.

Thomas moves forward out of the crowd, his hat in his hand.

"Sorry, Cap'n. We was just havin' some fun."

The mysterious captain. I sway on the rope and turn to look at him. He's a tall, broad man in a long coat and tri-corn hat. He has a greying beard and lines spreading from the corners of his eyes.

"Untie her. Immediately."

He moves in front of me and I'm suddenly even more aware of my nakedness. I can't cover myself. Tears stream down my cheeks and I sob uncontrollably. Someone behind me loosens the rope and my arms drop in front of me. The captain himself steps in to untie the knots. His face is shrouded in shadow and I can't make out his expression, but authority radiates from him.

My legs fail me and I stagger forwards. The captain catches

me and easily scoops me up into his arms.

He turns in a circle to address his men. "If any man lays a hand on this young woman, he will lose that hand. Have I made myself clear?"

A chorus of "Aye"s rumbles around the crowd.

The captain carries me effortlessly towards the stern. I cling to his coat, curling my body up against him. The murmurs of voices follow us as the crowd resumes its revels without me. I'm carried through the door that I was warned against entering and the captain and I are swallowed into his private quarters.

CHAPTER THREE

The room is lit by a single lantern hanging from the ceiling and swaying with the motion of the ship. A desk takes up nearly half the room, directly below the lantern. A huge map is stretched out on it, held down at the corners by large paper weights. Next to the desk is a large globe on a stand. On the other side of the room is a mahogany dining table set with four chairs. A candelabra is bolted to the centre of the table but the candles aren't lit. The remains of the captain's dinner—a plate with a few crumbs on it, some cutlery and crumpled napkin—rest at one end of the table.

I turn my face away from the cosy room, pressing it against his chest as he carries me through another door on the far side. He moves sideways through the narrow door into a dark room at the very stern of the ship. I peer cautiously out, wiping the tears from my eyes. It's a generously sized cabin with many windows all along the back wall and a large bed set between a wardrobe and a set of bookshelves.

The captain takes me to the bed and sits me gently on the side of it. I pull my feet up onto the bed, hugging my knees to my chest. He turns and opens a large trunk in front of the wardrobe, rummages inside it for a moment and returns to me with a large, white shirt. I take it from his outstretched hand and gingerly pull it over my head. Keeping my knees tucked against me, I pull the shirt over my legs too, hiding my body.

"Thank you," I croak with what little voice I can muster.

He sits on the bed beside me, not too close, and studies me with hard eyes. He discards his hat on the bed behind us.

"Are you injured?"

"No," I say, shaking my head. "Although my pride took a knock."

"I can't apologise enough. I did not authorise that behaviour."

I nod mutely, unable to meet his penetrating gaze.

"What's your name?"

"Hester."

"I'm Captain James Blackthorne. You can call me Jim. Did Briggs hire you?"

"Yes." My voice cracks and I cough to clear my throat. "I was working in a tavern in Charleston and he offered me a gold coin for every man aboard his ship if I'd come aboard." Fresh tears spill down my cheeks. "I didn't think it would be like that."

The captain scowls and shakes his head. "Briggs doesn't have that kind of wealth. Are you sure he offered you gold?"

I think over the conversation in the tavern. He was playing with a gold guinea. I have it tucked in my bag on my bunk even now. That one coin alone was more money than I'd seen at once in my life. But as the conversation replays in my mind, I realise my mistake. He was flashing gold at me, but—"He only said coin." I close my eyes and let out a groan. He could have meant a copper coin for all I knew. I just assumed gold.

"It's beside the point really," he says. "It still isn't right what just happened. We're a whole day out from port and a week away from our destination. I'm afraid I can't take you home."

"I understand."

"But..." He scrapes a hand over his bearded face. "I will pay you thirty gold coins when we reach Nassau and will protect you for the rest of the journey."

I blink at him, unsure I've heard him correctly.

"You can stay here in my cabin. No one will trouble you."

"That's very generous," I say, still shocked.

"It's the least I can do. Again, I am so sorry this happened to you."

Thirty guineas was still a vast amount of money. It would take me more than ten years to earn that as a barmaid. I don't fully believe he would pay me that much. I gaze at him in wide-eyed disbelief.

"I'll work for it," I say, lifting my chin. "I can't take that amount of gold to sit idle for a week. Besides, I'll lose my mind closeted up in this cabin for that long."

He nods, the corners of his eyes crinkling.

"Very well. There's plenty of work to go around. But I want you to be safe. I won't put you in harms way if I can help it."

"I understand. I won't go looking for trouble."

"You realise, Hester, that it isn't just my men that pose a risk to you? Just being at sea is perilous enough. But also, the nature of what we do, this crew, I mean. Have you gathered that yet?"

"You're pirates," I say, not meeting his gaze. "It doesn't take a week to reach Nassau from Charleston."

"No, it doesn't. We'll be taking a detour or two."

"I understand." I'd worked in that dockside tavern long enough to pick up a few things about what men like him did at sea. "I'll keep out of the way."

"Thank you. Now, I need to return to my men. Get some rest. Please take my bed for the duration of your stay." I glance around the room and see a hammock swinging by the windows. I look back at him and shake my head.

"I couldn't deprive you of your bed for that long. That thing can't be comfortable." I jerk my head towards the hammock.

"Have you ever slept in a hammock?" he asks, the corner of his mouth twitching.

I shake my head.

"Then you must take the bed. Trust me, my back can handle the hammock, but yours might not."

"Thank you, again."

He stands, scooping his hat from the bed as he does. He graces me with a slight bow before leaving the room. I shiver in the dark and cold. Cautiously, I lower my feet to the wooden floor and walk slowly around the end of the bed. The only light in the room is the faint glow under the door from the lamp in the study and a shimmer of silver moonlight through the vast windows. I tip-toe over to them and look at at the choppy, black sea behind the ship. The captain's quarters are surprisingly high and I fully appreciate the size of the ship as I gaze down into the waves below.

I wrap my arms around me and turn to look about the room properly. The books on the shelves beside the bed are held in place by fine, brass bars a couple of inches up from each shelf. It's too dark to make out the titles. The hammock hangs from the wall beside the window to one of two wooden pillars in the middle of the room. It swings with the motion of the ship. On the other side of the hammock is a narrow door, beside it is a wooden cabinet with a ceramic basin fastened to it. I approach and see milky-white water half-filling the deep basin, sloshing gently from side to side. I open the little door a crack and see a narrow privy. I quickly close it again, wrinkling my nose automatically, although it doesn't smell. I return to the basin and breathe in the scent of soap. I can't help glancing around to check that I really am alonc. On confirming it, I lift thc captain's shirt off and dip my hands into the cool water. I splash my face and brace myself against the cold. Carefully, I freshen myself up in all the important places and look for a towel. I open the cabinet below the basin and find a neat stack of folded towels there. I take one out and pat myself dry, then hang the towel over a brass rail and put the shirt back on. It hangs loosely over my petite frame, brushing the tops of my thighs. The lace-up neck hangs open, exposing my ample cleavage. But it covers most of me well enough.

I return to the bed and fold back the crisp white linens, slipping beneath them with a sigh. I don't know the hour, only that my body feels wrung out from the long, strange day. The down-filled pillows cradle my head as I close my eyes, but sleep doesn't come easily. My thoughts spin, tangled with questions and unspoken feelings. Still, the ship rocks gently beneath me, its motion familiar now, comforting. Just as the last threads of wakefulness begin to fade, I hear it—soft footsteps outside the door. A pause. Then silence.

CHAPTER FOUR

It's still dark when my eyes slowly peel open. The captain is lying in the hammock across the room, his bare feet hanging out either side. He's in his clothes, but his boots stand on the floor beneath him. I sit up in the bed and rub my face. I turn and lower my feet to the floor. My bag sits on the floor near the foot of the bed. I smile, knowing the captain must have retrieved it from the bunk I'd been given earlier.

Planting my feet and feeling the motion of the ship before I attempt to stand, I make my way over to the bank of windows. A shiver runs through my body. The moon has moved away and its glow barely lights the room now. I turn to head back to bed and catch sight of the captain in his hammock. His eyes are open and fixed on me. We gaze at each other for a moment that seems to extend beyond the few seconds that it must surely be.

A lump rises in my throat. Seeing him stretched out, his legs spread to hang out of the hammock like that. His shirt is undone, exposing a portion of his chest. His breeches are loosened too and I look away.

"Sorry," I mutter. "I didn't mean to wake you."

I scurry back to the bed. He doesn't say a word but he shifts in the hammock to lie on his side facing the bed. I curl up, my back to the vast window and close my eyes, eager to return to sleep.

A soft thud behind me causes my eyes to pop open.

I turn my head to see him standing beside the hammock, straightening his clothing. He steps to the window and places his left hand on the wooden frame, leaning casually as he gazes out to sea. I watch him, fascinated by this polite, almost gentlemanly man who for some reason captains a vessel full of pirate scum. I roll over to get a better look at him. He's very tall, well over six feet, and his shoulders are broad. His imposing frame would make him stand out in any crowd. But on top of that, he's strikingly handsome, for an older man. I honestly couldn't place his age accurately, but the streaks of grey in his hair and beard, and the lines at the corners of his eyes made him look distinguished and probably twice my age of one and twenty.

"It's almost dawn," he says, his voice quiet but rough with sleep.

I take a breath and get out of bed again. I move over to stand beside him and he lowers his arm from the window frame. He moves behind me and gently takes me by the shoulders, turning me to the right slightly. His warm body is almost pressed against my back I suck in a breath. On the horizon, the faintest pink glow has appeared.

"I see it," I whisper, afraid of what my voice will do. He's still standing too close to me for polite company. His hands run gently down my arms, lightly caressing them through the thin cotton shirt. Oh. This is happening.

Goosebumps break out on my arms and it has nothing to do with the chill in the air.

He moves his hands to my hips, holding them lightly. His breath is warm on my hair. His fingers tentatively lift the shirt and a gasp escapes my lips. He instantly releases the shirt and steps back.

“I apologise.” He turns and strides towards the door to the study.

“You don't have to go!” I call after him, turning to face him.

“I shouldn't have done that.” He stops, one hand on the door handle, his face turned slightly to his left. “It wouldn't be proper under normal circumstances, let alone after last night.” He opens the door and closes it firmly behind him.

Frustration rushes through my veins. His attention is welcome, despite everything. In fact, what I need most after being threatened so cruelly, is the gentle touch of a good man. I crave reassurance.

I stride after him and fling the door wide. He's sitting at his desk, his chair pushed back and his bare feet crossed at the ankles. He looks up at me, startled.

“I'm not a maiden!” I snap at him, heat rising in my cheeks. “I'm not a lady. I'm not innocent. I've worked in taverns since I was fifteen years old. Men have seen themselves entitled to have their way with me ever since. Some advances were less welcome than others, I'll admit. But I've known the first love of youth in amongst the lecherous old men who've used me. Girls like me don't concern themselves with what's ‘proper’. I came aboard this ship knowing in my heart what Briggs was suggesting and I came willingly. Would an innocent girl do that? So if you want me, get back in here and have me.” I point to the floor in the bedroom before turning on my heel and flouncing back inside. I can't quite believe what I've done and I raise my hands to my temples. I make it over to the windows before his voice halts me.

“What do you want?” I turn to see him standing in the doorway, lit from behind by the lantern swinging from the ceiling.

“What do you mean?” I cross my arms over my chest. No

man has ever asked me that before.

"Well, you had a lot to say just then." He shifts his weight and fixes his dark eyes on my face. "About how men have used you. I witnessed my own men prepared to rape you to death last night." There's a dangerous edge to his voice, a flared temper where before I'd only seen kindness. "That doesn't sit right with me and it shouldn't with you either. Do you really want another lecherous old man to use you? Or do you want to be treated with dignity and respect?"

I blanch at that. I look away. Heat rises in my cheeks and my emotions threaten to get the best of me.

"I really want to know, Hester." When I return my gaze to him, he's crossing the room towards me. His voice has softened.

"You aren't a lecherous old man." I say, grumbling to the floor at my feet. "You're really quite handsome."

"I must be twice your age." He's right in front of me now and I look up into his bearded face. "How old are you?"

"One and twenty."

"Well that does it, I am almost twice your age and I won't treat you like a whore, even if that is how you are used to being treated. I won't lay a hand on you without your express permission."

He turns and strides for the door again.

"You have it, Jim. For goodness sake. That's what I'm saying."

He reaches the door and looks back over his shoulder at me. I plant my hands on my hips and lift my chin. He slams the door and crosses the room in four deep strides. He takes hold of my face and captures my lips with his. He walks me backwards and I bump into the glass behind me as he ravishes my mouth, his tongue probing deeply. My hands grip his waist and find their way under his shirt to his hot skin. He returns my advance by pressing his body hard against me. I'm sandwiched between the cold glass and his warm body. I gasp between frantic kisses, desperate to draw breath.

He breaks contact for a moment to yank his shirt up over his head. I take a second to run my gaze over his chiselled torso. His chest and stomach are well muscled and covered with dark hair leading down... I reach for the buttons of his breeches. The top ones are already undone but I make short work of the rest. The large bulge in beneath the thick cotton suggest that he is large everywhere.

He takes hold of my wrists, halting me. He presses himself against me again and I feel the hardness of him pressing into me. His dark eyes rake over my lips.

"You should know that I don't normally do this."

"No," I say with a smirk. "Because it isn't proper."

"Exactly."

"What kind of a pirate are you?" I let a grin spread across my lips.

"Right now, an eager one." He kisses me again, still holding my wrists firmly in his hands. He raises my hands over my head, pinning them with one hand against the window. His other hand trails down my front, over one breast and down to the hem of his shirt. He slips his hand under the cotton and finds the spot where my thighs meet my body. I gasp as his fingers spread the soft lips there. With practised ease, he finds the sweet, sensitive bud. Our eyes are locked onto one another as he begins to slowly circle it with his callused fingers. I draw a breath and clamp my lower lip between my teeth.

His fingers slip past that most sensitive place and two of them slide inside me. I close my eyes and drop my head back against the glass with a whimper. His lips caress my neck as he works his fingers inside my wet entrance. I've never been touched like this, never felt heat like this. I breathe heavily, my head swims.

He adds a third finger and moves them slowly in and out of me, testing me, I think, seeing what I can take. My mind is a swirling mess of sensation and fractured thoughts and memories. Pleasure bursts within me in new and unexpected ways. I moan as the wave reaches its peak.

He releases my hands and they fall onto his shoulders. He captures my mouth in a deep and probing kiss again, swallowing my cries of pleasure. He eases his fingers out of me and breaks the kiss to swiftly pull the shirt off over my head. I yank at his breeches, tugging them over his hips.

"I have to have you inside me right now," I whisper. He helps me to shed his clothes and stands before me naked and rock hard. His manhood is significantly larger than any I've seen before and for a moment I doubt if it will fit inside me. He glances down at it, seeming to know my thoughts. "It's like a rolling pin," I say in awe.

"I'll be gentle," he says, moving closer to me. I nod and take him into my arms. Once again, he presses me against the glass. It's cold against my bare skin but all I feel is his heat.

He grabs hold of my legs behind my knees and hitches me up, my skin squeaking against the window. I hold tight to his shoulders and marvel at his strength. His cock rests between us, twitching slightly as he kisses my neck. Holding me firmly, he pulls back and positions himself to enter me. The head of his impressive tool eases into me and I hold my breath, gazing down to watch as he slides it slowly, one inch at a time into my slick passage. He goes slowly, checking my face for signs of discomfort, but all I feel is incredible pleasure and pressure. It's a tight fit, but as he glides deeper in, the fit feels better and better.

We both watch as the gap between us closes and finally,

he's fully sheathed inside me. He adjusts his grip on my thighs and presses his torso against mine. My breasts smoosh against his firm chest and he begins to move in me. I thread my fingers together at the back of his neck and cross my ankles across his buttocks.

"Are you all right?" He asks tenderly.

I don't seem to be able to form words. I nod and grin.

I feel him inside me, moving and throbbing. His thrusts are slow and gentle. He holds my gaze, his face serious.

This is very different from the alley walls I've been fucked against more times than I can count. There's such intensity in his eyes, burning passion there. This isn't just an opportunistic tumble. He cares about my pleasure. I've never had that, even with the young man I loved and thought to marry. We were young and inexperienced and as long as he spilled his seed on my stomach or back, it was done. He'd been whipped hard by his father for toying with me and after a few weeks I never saw him again.

I look into Jim's eyes and a surge of something I don't understand rushes up from my stomach into my throat. I might mistake it for nausea, but that isn't quite it. Intense pleasure like a wave cascades through my whole body. It's sexual desire mingled with an emotional release. I feel safe, I feel desired, I feel longing for the man inside me. It's new and frightening and a cry bursts from my throat, guttural and primal.

"Are you still well?" he asks, coming to a halt as he searches my face.

"Yes," I gasp. "I've never, I don't know what this is."

He presses me hard against the glass, pinning me in place as he releases one thigh to caress my cheek. I realise a tear has fallen. He wipes it away with his thumb and kisses the cheek.

"We can stop."

"No," I say, clinging tight to him. "More, I need more. Harder, faster."

With no more words, he resumes the rocking of his hips, deepening his thrusts. I look up at the ceiling. It's tinted orange with the golden glow rising behind me. A cry escapes my mouth again as another surge of pleasure rushes through me. He picks up the pace even more, spurred on by my obvious enjoyment.

His thrusts become sharper with more space and cool air between our groins with each outward motion. A whimper rushes from me with every thrust and he begins to match my vocalisations with grunts of his own. His hands firmly grip my buttocks as he rams into me again and again, fucking me harder like I asked. Our eyes meet for a moment before I look down between our bodies again to watch.

His cock glistens with my juices as it emerges from me, only to slam back into me. I'm fascinated by the motion and keep my gaze locked onto our coupled bodies.

"Fuck," I say as another wave crashes upon me. I throw my head back, slamming it hard against the glass. "Yes!" This time my voice is an outright shout.

"More?" he asks, his breathing ragged.

"Yes, more!"

He pounds at me, slamming me repeatedly against the window. I explode inside. Every muscle tenses and my fingers dig into his shoulders so hard that my nails draw blood. He winces but is undeterred. With a mighty groan, his hips jerk, suddenly breaking his steady rhythm. He yanks back, pulling swiftly out of me but holding me in place as his seed spills onto the wooden floor between his feet.

I gasp for breath, whimpering and moaning as pleasure continues to course through me. We're both shaking as he carefully lowers me to the floor, making sure I don't stand in his spilled seed. A fine sheen of sweat covers my skin as well as his. I stumble forwards, unable to stand unassisted. I chuckle and rest my head against his chest.

"Here," he says, guiding me to the bed. We both collapse on it, our limbs tangling together. He kisses the top of my head and wraps an arm around me, drawing me onto his chest. "That was incredible."

"It was," I whisper. Golden dawn covers our bodies as we lay there. "I don't have the words for it."

"Me neither." He kisses my head again. "It's been a year or more since I was inside a woman. Not many can take all of me."

"I'm not surprised," I say, chuckling again. "It's a beast. I suppose I'm special."

"Very." He caresses my shoulder with his hand. His voice is deadly serious. My body stills as I consider the words passing between us. I wonder what it is that I'm feeling. And if he feels it too.

CHAPTER FIVE

Jim rolls away from me and gets to his feet. He heads for the basin to freshen up and I lie there on my side, watching his beautiful, naked body move in the pinkish gold light of dawn. He pats himself dry with the towel I used last night and moves back in my direction. His face is all stern again as he passes alongside the bed and heads for his trunk. He fishes out fresh clothes for the day and I watch him dress, a dizzy smile lingering on my full lips.

Once he finishes tucking his clean, white shirt into his brown trousers, he turns to me, plants his hands on the bed and leans down to kiss me.

"Stay here, naked, just like this and I'll be back as soon as possible to do that to you again."

"Sounds perfect," I say, my voice a little husky. I capture one of his hands as he starts to pull away and instead tug him closer, planting his hand on my breast. He obliges by squeezing it gently then flicking his thumb over my raised nipple.

"Later," he whispers, pulling free and stepping towards the door. "Don't get dressed. I mean it."

"Yes Cap'n," I say with a grin. He glances over his shoulder at me and then disappears through the door.

"Mornin', Cap'n," a voice calls from the next room. My face

drops as I recognise Briggs's voice. Jim closes the door with a firm click and their conversation is nothing but mumbles through the solid wooden door and wall. I don't even try to listen. I don't want to know. I wonder how many men heard my cries but swiftly put it out of my mind.

I slide off the bed and potter around the room. I make use of the privy, which isn't as bad as I feared it might be, then have a wash at the basin. In the cabinet, I find a rag and use it to clean the floor where Jim made a mess. I knew some of how it all worked and had done my best throughout my life to avoid men pumping their fluid into me, at least down there. So far, I'd managed to not find myself with child. Shaking away such thoughts, I busy myself. I discover a jug of fresh water in a cupboard beside the bed and pour myself a mug. I'm thirstier than I thought possible and after downing the mug in one, I pour another and repeat the motion.

I open the wardrobe and find it empty, so I take it upon myself to unpack Jim's trunk into the wardrobe and matching chest of drawers. He has plenty of shirts and undergarments, though I note that he wasn't wearing the latter when he stripped this morning. In the bottom of the trunk is a locked, wooden box, which piques my curiosity. I leave it in place, deciding he probably wouldn't want me moving it. I then turn to my own bag. I tug the inside of one cheek between my teeth, wondering if it's too presumptuous to unpack my own things into his furniture. Deciding there's little option, I go ahead and hang up my things. He has plenty of space.

A gentle knock at the door catches me off guard and my gaze snaps towards it.

"It's me," Jim's voice calls through the door. He opens it and slips inside. He casts his gaze around the room before landing on me, standing in front of his near-empty trunk and now-full wardrobe. A frown creases his brow. "You unpacked?"

"Is that all right?"

He moves over to me, places a gentle hand on my waist and kisses my cheek.

"Perfectly. Thank you." His gaze flickers to my empty bag on the floor and my dresses hanging in the wardrobe. The corner of his mouth twitches. "You unpacked your things too. I take it that means you're happy to stay here with me?"

"Hmm, let me think. Stay in this large and comfortable room with plenty of light and total privacy, or return to the tiny bunk wedged between barrels of salted fish in the middle of a corridor filled with dirty rapists. Tough choice really."

Even that doesn't raise a laugh from him. I thought it was pretty funny. But no, he frowns even more deeply.

"I had young Ben flogged."

"Oh," I say, startled by his directness.

"I knew last night that it would have to happen, but I wanted him sober when Briggs did it."

"I see. Thank you."

"Half the crew saw. Everyone will know by now. That should help to protect you, so you can move about the ship. I don't want to keep you cooped up in here unnecessarily. You said you didn't want to be idle."

"I did. Thank you." I feel like I'll be saying that a lot.

"Anyway, I brought breakfast. You can put some clothes on to eat in there if you like." He jerks his head towards his study.

"How thoughtful." I grin at him. "How about I just put your shirt back on?"

"That suits me." I pick up the shirt I wore last night from where I'd laid it at the end of the bed and slip it on over my head. I roll up the sleeves and pad barefoot to the door, which he holds open for me. "I'm afraid it's only porridge. But I have something, well two somethings, that they don't have in the galley." He holds back a chair for me and I sit before a steaming bowl of thick porridge - a better consistency than the stuff I served yesterday. He leans past me and lifts the lid on a small jar in the middle of the table. A small spoon handle sticks out from it and he lifts it to show me shining, golden honey drizzling from it.

"Ooh!" I coo with delight.

"And..." He opens a small barrel on a shelf and scoops out a handful of mixed berries. He scatters them onto my porridge and I eagerly dollop some honey on top of the lot.

"This is lovely!" I grin before lifting my spoon and tucking in.

He sits at the head of the table in front of his own bowl and begins to eat. I'm afraid my table manners dessert me. I eat like a starving whelp and make no apology for it. It's been at least fifteen hours since any food passed my lips and that was only a small helping of broth before the dinner rush in the galley. I glance sideways at the captain. He sits leaning back in his chair, poking at his breakfast with his spoon, his gaze fixed on me. I swallow a mouthful of food and smile weakly at him. His mouth twitches slightly again. I decide then and there to make it my life's mission to make him smile. I finish my breakfast more slowly and keep half an eye on him as he eats.

He pushes his bowl aside and reaches out to take my hand. He squeezes it and rubs the back of it with his thumb.

"I have no appetite," he says in a low voice. "Least, not that kind."

He tugs my hand firmly and I allow him to pull me from my chair and into his lap. His erection strains at his trousers and presses into my thigh.

"Did watching me eat like an animal get you excited?" I ask, stroking his beard.

"Apparently so. I certainly want to do very carnal things to you right now." His hand moves up my thigh and squeezes my hip. He tugs his shirt out from under my bottom and spins me on his lap so that my back is pressed against his chest. "Are you ready for more?" he asks as he runs his callused hands up under the shirt and over my breasts. He takes hold of both of them and kneads them firmly. I moan and grind my hips against him.

"Absolutely," I whisper.

He gets to his feet, tossing me out of his lap. I stumble forwards and thrust my hands out to stop me from crashing into his desk. He grabs hold of my hips and runs his hands up over my back, pushing the shirt up and exposing my skin.

"Exactly what I have in mind." His voice is a low rumble from his chest. He runs his fingers across my sex and dips them into me, getting me wet.

He unfastens his trousers with his free hand and I tease him with gentle sways of my hips. I'm eager for a repeat performance. He slides three fingers into me and pushes them apart, widening my passage. He slips them out, leans forward and rubs them over my right nipple, spreading my wetness across the sensitive skin there. I let a small whimper escape my lips.

His rock hard cock presses into my behind while he plays with my nipple some more. I grind my hips impatiently against his firm grip.

Taking my cue, he takes hold of my left hip and guides his manhood into me with his right hand. I gasp. He's less gradual this time, now he knows I can take it. He slides right into me, pressing his groin against my backside. My hands grip the edge of the desk. The shirt I'm wearing has been pushed right up my body and is bunched up around my shoulders. My breasts hang beneath me, swaying as he begins to thrust.

His right hand goes to the small of my back and pushes it

down, forcing my spine into a deep curve. He swiftly reaches for my hair with his right hand, grabs a fistful of it and tugs my head back.

I gasp hard, surprised by his sudden roughness. But I like it. Excitement rushes up inside me and a cry bursts from my mouth. I quickly stifle it, knowing there is far more chance of being heard in here than in the bedroom, which is further from the men on deck.

He picks up the pace while holding me firmly in place with his left hand on my hip and his right hand tangled in my hair. A pounding rhythm matches my short, sharp breaths. His balls slap noisily against me with every thrust. My legs begin to shake as the pleasure becomes too much. My mouth hangs open as I hold my ecstatic cries at bay.

“Fuck, this feels good,” he says softly behind me, his voice almost lost against the wet noises of our coupling.

The door to the deck bursts open and I shout in shock as Briggs fills the doorway. But the captain doesn’t stop. He continues fucking me. If anything, his thrusts get harder and quicker. Hurt and confusion override my pleasure and I fumble with the shirt to cover my breasts.

“Sorry to interrupt, Cap’n,” Briggs says with a frown, swiftly replaced by a dirty leer at my body.

“What the fuck do you want?” The captain releases my hair and grips my hips tightly in both hands, pumping his hips vigorously.

“Lookout’s spotted a vessel off our port bow.”

“Terrible timing,” the captain grunts, but still he continues.

I don’t know what to do except let it happen. Hurt wells in me and I begin to cry. I can’t help the tears. Was it all a lie before?

“Keep an eye on it and keep pace with it, but don’t get too

close. We won't go in until we confirm what ship it is. I'll be there in five—make it ten minutes. Get out."

"Aye Cap'n." Briggs steps out and slams the door.

Jim instantly releases me, pulls out of me and spins me to face him.

"I am so gravely sorry for that." He pulls me against him and holds me while I sob into his chest, my shoulders shaking. "The men all know you're in here with me. I can't appear sentimental. Do you see that? I can't have them see me differently than they did yesterday. They have to think that I saved you last night to use for myself."

I pull away from him and slap him hard across the face. My lip trembles.

"You set it up. Didn't you? You knew he'd come in here and you wanted him to see that."

"I did."

"You could have told me what you needed and I would have put on a show for you, you bastard. What happened to dignity and respect?" I storm away into the bedroom and slam the door.

CHAPTER SIX

I pace the bedroom, my fists clenched as fury pounds in my veins. My right palm aches from slapping him. A small part of me actually hopes to see him come through that door to apologise and make it up to me. But he doesn't. I'm alone. Tears sting my eyes and I swat them away as they fall. With resolve, I get dressed and do my hair. I swing open the door and find his study empty. The breakfast things are still on the table. I don't know if there's someone whose job it is to clear the captain's table, but I take it upon myself to do it. I notice that his porridge is still largely untouched. With a resigned sigh, I pick out the fruit to eat before stacking his bowl on top of mine and dumping the spoons into the top bowl.

I open the door onto the deck and bright sunlight greets me. The air is humid. A tell tale sign that we've travelled quite a distance south of Charleston. The deck bustles with men and a jolly sea shanty rings on the air, in stark contrast to my dark mood. I peek cautiously around but see no familiar faces. I tighten my grip on the breakfast things and stride across the deck to the door at the opposite end of the ship. No one stops me, I just receive a few curious glances. I open the door and step into the shade of the bow corridor. I make my way past burly sailors to the galley and squeeze through the gap into the kitchen. Cook looks me up and down with surprise.

"You're back."

"Of course," I say, coolly. "There's work to be done." I drop the bowls onto a large stack of dishes and roll up my sleeves. Cook gives me an appraising look and tosses me an apron. I put it on and get to work.

I clean every dish, frequently swiping back stray hair from my sweaty face. I scrub the floor and mend a tear in Cook's apron while he sits playing cards with some of the men. I don't mind the work. It keeps my hands and mind occupied. As I finish the mending and get to my feet, I catch sight of young Ben sitting at a bench on the opposite side of the galley. Our eyes meet and he hurriedly looks away. His back is hunched and as a passing shipmate thumps him hard on it, he winces and the other man laughs. I'm not sorry that he's in pain. The scoundrel deserves it.

Cook gets back to work as lunchtime rolls around and I serve the men that file through seeking food. There's banter and jokes aplenty, but no one speaks to me. They cast wary glances my way and I catch several men leering at me and talking about me with their fellows. I pretend not to notice and get on with my work.

I'm curious about the ship that was sighted at breakfast, but nothing seems to have come of it. Just as it crosses my mind, I overhear two men talking about it as they hold their plates out to me to dollop mashed potatoes onto.

"It was a Navy vessel, 'parently," one of them says. "Cap'n ordered us to change course to avoid it."

"Dare say we'll catch up to the Sea Devil soon enough."

They move away and out of earshot. Avoiding the Navy and tracking down a specific ship, are we? I consider that for a moment until I'm dragged out of my thoughts to serve another sailor. He gives me a small smile and a nod as he moves away, which is more than most of them offer.

The afternoon passes slowly, with not much to do. I head back up on deck to feel the sun on my face. I lean against the bulwark, letting the steady roll of the ship rock me gently. The sea stretches endless and blue before me, shimmering beneath the afternoon sun. A warm breeze brushes across my face, leaving the taste of salt on my lips and ruffling stray wisps of my hair. I close my eyes, breathing deeply, allowing the tension in my shoulders to melt away bit by bit.

For the first time since stepping aboard The Stormchaser, I feel something close to peace. The sounds of the crew blend into the rhythmic lull of the waves, their laughter distant, unimportant. I focus instead on the steady creak of the ship's timbers, the snap of sails overhead. There is a freedom in the sea that I hadn't anticipated—a vastness that makes my anger feel small, insignificant.

I think of the captain, of his harsh words, his cold demeanour. Of the way his eyes darkened with something almost like regret before I struck him. The memory makes my stomach twist. I had every right to be furious, and yet...

A sigh escapes my lips.

I hadn't known what to expect from him, but I certainly hadn't anticipated this complicated mess of emotions. He's not what I had imagined a pirate captain to be. There's something contained about him, something reserved. Not cruel, but distant—burdened. And, for all my anger, I can't ignore the fact that he had let me go unpunished. He could have locked me away, cast me out to fend for myself. Instead, he left me to my own devices, as though trusting me to decide for myself what comes next.

I shift my weight against the bulwark, tracing the worn

wood beneath my fingers.

Maybe I was too quick to strike him. Maybe I should have let him explain. Maybe, despite everything, I don't hate him as much as I want to.

I hear boots against the deck behind me and straighten instinctively, wiping the sweat from my brow. Thomas Briggs strolls past, casting me a sidelong glance before leaning on the rail beside me. "Didn't think I'd see you up here, looking so at ease."

I shrug, unwilling to admit that I was beginning to feel the ship's pull on me, that I was coming to understand why men chose the sea over land.

"Sun feels good," I say simply. I try to ignore the humiliation I feel at facing this man who has seen me in the most compromising position. I long for him to leave me alone.

He chuckles. "Aye, it does at that." He nods toward the horizon. "Best enjoy it while it lasts. We'll be pushing hard after the Sea Devil soon enough. No telling how long the chase'll take." He saunters away, leaving me to my thoughts.

I nod to myself, my fingers curling against the wood. A pursuit. A hunt. The idea unsettles me, but I say nothing. Instead, I let the breeze carry away my doubts, at least for now.

I try to let go of my anger. Not entirely, but enough to breathe easier beneath the wide open sky.

With a deep breath, I push away from the bulwark and make my way below deck. The galley is warm and thick with the scent of simmering broth and baking bread. Cook glances up as I step inside, one bushy eyebrow raised.

"What's for the captain's dinner?" I ask, wiping my hands on my skirt.

He snorts. "Got a fine salmon on ice. Was thinkin' of boiling it up."

I wrinkle my nose at the thought. "Let me cook it."

Cook narrows his eyes but shrugs, gesturing toward the fish with a flick of his knife. "Suit yourself. But make it worth the trouble."

I roll up my sleeves, searching through the meagre stores for anything to elevate the meal. A few firm potatoes, a pat of butter wrapped in cloth, a handful of fresh mint, and—miraculously—two lemons. It's enough. I set to work, gutting and cleaning the salmon, then seasoning it generously before placing it over the fire with the potatoes. The warm scent of butter and citrus soon fills the galley, drawing a few curious glances from passing crew members.

By the time the fish is cooked to perfection, golden and steaming, I wipe the sweat from my brow and straighten. Now, the final task—getting it to the captain's table.

I glance at two nearby deckhands, men I recognize but have never spoken to. Summoning my courage, I step toward them. "I need help carrying this up to the captain's cabin."

The men exchange glances, then nod without protest. One grabs the heavy platter, the other the side dishes, and together we make our way to the captain's quarters. I take a steadying breath before stepping inside, setting to work laying the table, making sure everything is placed just so.

Not yet satisfied, I reach for the small flint box resting on the shelf. My fingers tremble slightly as I strike it, lighting the tall, thin candles in the candelabra bolted to the middle of the table. The warm glow flickers over the polished wood, casting soft shadows across the cabin. Once finished, I step back, surveying my work. The cabin is quiet, save for the distant sounds of the ship's movement. I smooth my hands over my apron and wait.

The door creaks open, and I turn as Captain Blackthorne steps inside. His eyes sweep over the table, the golden salmon glistening under the candlelight, the carefully arranged settings, and finally, me. His expression flickers with something unreadable—surprise, perhaps even gratitude. He removes his hat, hanging it on the peg by the door before shrugging off his coat and hanging it beside his hat.

He exhales, running a hand through his hair before sitting at the table. "I wasn't expecting this," he murmurs, voice quieter than usual.

I hesitate for only a moment before stepping forward. "You should eat while it's warm."

He nods, picking up his knife, but then pauses, glancing at me. "Sit."

I blink, startled by the offer, but obey, lowering myself into the chair to his right. The warm glow of the candles dances across his features as he studies me for a moment, then reaches across the table, taking my hand in his roughened grasp.

"I owe you an apology," he says, his thumb grazing over my knuckles. "For my words, for my actions. You were within your rights to strike me."

My breath catches slightly, caught off guard by the sincerity in his voice. I let the moment settle between us, unspoken understanding filling the space where anger once lingered.

He releases my hand and tucks into the fish. "Did you cook this?" he asks, lifting an eyebrow.

"I did. Cook was planning to boil it." I shudder. "This fine salmon deserved better than that."

"Well, I'm certainly grateful. Don't tell him this, but I'm tired to the back teeth of him boiling everything." I chuckle and check his face for a hint of a smile. Still nothing.

"I heard talk today of a ship we're pursuing. The Sea Devil?" I lift my fork to my mouth and take a bite as I watch him for his reply. He nods, finishing a mouthful of food.

"That's right."

"Is that a merchant ship?"

"No," he says, pausing to assess me. "Why do you want to know?"

"I'm just curious," I reply before taking another bite of fish. He nods and continues eating, not answering right away.

"I'm cautious of putting you in a difficult position."

"Oh, don't worry, I excel at those." I smirk and cock my eyebrows at him, hoping he'll take the bait.

He fixes his icy stare on me and the smirk disappears from my face. What's it going to take to crack this man?

"The Sea Devil is captained by Gideon Kane, a most unsavoury man. He has something I want. We're going after him to get it."

"Oh. What is it? Gold? A treasure map? A family heirloom?"

"Stop asking so many questions. I already asked you to stay out of it. I don't want you to get hurt." He tucks into his food and there is a finality to his words that I accept. I eat quietly, chancing frequent glances at him.

When we finish eating he wipes his hands and mouth on a napkin and gets to his feet. He takes my hand and leads me over to his desk. He straightens the map and examines it with his arm around my waist.

"We're here," he says, pointing at a stretch of sea off the east coast of a pointy bit of land. "This is where we're going, where the Sea Devil is heading." He points at a group of islands just north of Nassau. "We should be there in two days, but we might get lucky and intercept the Sea Devil sooner. My ship is faster."

"What I heard there is that we have two days to play with ourselves, or each other." I turn towards him and wrap one arm around his back, the other slides down his front and into his trousers.

"That may be the case, yes," he says, his voice a throaty rumble.

I un-tuck his shirt and slide my hand back down the front of his breeches and inside his underwear. My fingers find their target. He's just starting to firm up. He looks down into my hungry eyes and captures my mouth in a deep kiss. My hand wraps around him and begins to work him into a rock hard erection. I pull out my hand and break the kiss. Deftly, I unbutton his trousers and tug them over his hips. He lets me do what I will, his deep eyes fixed on me.

I firmly shove him into the chair behind his desk and look down at his dick standing up tall and ready. I lick my lips and drop to my knees. His arms rest on the arms of his chair and he watches me shrewdly as I get myself into position. I wrap my right hand around the shaft and lock my eyes onto his as I take the head of his cock into my mouth. I've had a lot of compliments on this particular skill in my time and I approach it with confidence.

I work his foreskin back, exposing the head fully. I run my tongue all the way around the head, keeping my gaze on his eyes. He watches me with equal intensity.

His eyes flicker closed for a second before springing open again and fixing back on mine.

"I'm expecting company soon. I have to meet with my men."

I don't answer, I just keep sucking like his cock is an ice pop on a hot day. My hand firmly working the length.

"I don't want a repeat of earlier," he says, his voice hoarse and slightly broken.

But I'm the one in control this time and I'm resolved to serve my Captain. So what if his men enter the room? He's the captain and he can conduct a meeting while being sucked off by his companion if he wants.

There's a sharp knock on the door and he stiffens in his chair. He tries to push me off him but I pin him in place and he doesn't use force.

"Just a minute!" he calls to whoever is on the other side of the door. "Hester, stop." He insists.

I pull off him and scowl at him. "No fun," I say with a sly wink. He gets to his feet, hurriedly tucking himself back into this clothes. I get to my feet, stride to the door and open it while wiping my hand across my mouth. A group of five of his senior crew, including Briggs stands at the door, looking confused. "Come on in gents," I say. I glance back at the flustered Captain. His erection can still be seen through his trousers and I press my lips together to stop myself from laughing.

The men file in, looking uncomfortable. I gather up the dinner things as they begin their meeting under an awkward shroud. I leave the room with the plates stacked neatly on one arm and close the door behind me. I set off for the galley, feeling satisfied by my little act of revenge.

CHAPTER SEVEN

I pat my hands dry after washing up the dinner things and Cook gives me leave to go. The sun is setting as I set foot up on deck and the sky is a wash of crimson and gold. The sea gently throbs with awesome power and reflects the stunning colours of the sky. I climb the steep steps up to the forecastle and make my way to the very front of the ship. I lean out over the bowsprit. The wind whips my hair out of its loose tie and I shake it out behind me. My skirt flaps about my legs and I feel as though I'm flying. There are a few deckhands nearby, but they go about their work and leave me alone.

Heavy footsteps thud up the steps and across the deck and I recognise the weight of them. A smile lights my face as the man approaches me. My Captain. His warm body presses against my back and his large hands settle on my shoulders.

"Here you are," he says, almost in a growl, at my ear. His breath is warm on my cheek. He kisses me softly.

"I hope your meeting was productive," I say, tilting my head to look him in the eye, but his gaze is set on the horizon ahead.

"Hmm," he murmurs. His hands run down my arms and around my waist, coming to rest on my belly. We stand like that, gazing out to sea, in easy silence for the longest time. I don't even mind the chill from the strong wind because I'm warm in his arms. I feel at peace and, judging my the way he relaxes against me, he does too. This is where he's most at home. The sun dips below the western horizon, off to starboard and the last blaze of gold shimmers across the churning sea.

"Come. We have matters to attend to in my cabin." He steps away from me and threads his fingers through mine to lead me the length of the ship. Men scurry out of his path, tipping their hats to him. We reach the door to his quarters and he pauses beside a young man in a knitted jumper. "No one is to disturb us unless it's an emergency. Is that clear?"

"Aye Cap'n."

Jim opens the door and holds it open for me, releasing my hand so that I can go through first. He closes the door behind us and clicks a bolt across it.

I turn to face him and begin unbuttoning my dress. I give him my most sultry pout.

"Where would you like to have me, Captain?"

He slips out of his jacket and hangs it, along with his hat, on their hook by the door. He moves towards me like a wild cat stalking his prey, unbuttoning his breeches.

"I'm still trying to decide. After the stunt you pulled earlier I've half a mind to throw you over my lap and spank you until you're raw."

I catch my lower lip between my teeth in eager anticipation.

"But you might enjoy that too much," he says, eyeing me carefully. He slips his trousers down and steps out of them. I slide my dress off my shoulders and let it pool on the floor around my feet. I stand before him in a cream bodice, my breasts heaving out of the top, and matching cream stockings. He rakes his gaze up and down my body, admiring my ample curves with wanton lust in his dark eyes. He tugs his shirt off over his head and resumes stalking towards me. I back slowly towards the bedroom door, kicking off my shoes as I go.

He follows me slowly into the bedroom and closes the door behind him.

"Get on the bed," he says, his voice a low rumble. I do as I'm told and sit down, moving myself backwards across the large bed. He's naked now and his manhood is standing to attention. I will never tire of seeing that magnificent piece of equipment, seemingly made specifically to fit me. He takes hold of it and strokes it a few time as he looks me up and down. "Take off your stockings." I keep eye contact as I follow his order. I toss the stockings away. "And your underwear." I wriggle out of my pantelettes and lean back on my hands, crossing my ankles. He continues to stroke himself as he watches me. "Touch yourself."

Heat rises in my cheeks. That isn't something I'm accustomed to doing. I uncross my ankles and plant my feet on the bed, my knees crooked and exposing myself completely for him. Nervously, I reach between my thighs. He takes a step closer, glancing down at himself before fixing his gaze back on my fingers as they circle my entrance. I skim over that hard bud between my nether lips and gasp at the sensation. It felt just like that when he touched me there.

"Very good," he whispers, moving closer still. "Now, put a finger inside."

I follow his instruction and slide my middle finger into myself. My breath quickens. This is a revelation! Little pulses of pleasure rush through me and my head drops back. I pump my finger slowly and carefully, feeling every fold and curve of flesh in there.

Jim kneels on the floor beside the bed and yanks me closer to him. I gasp and drop onto my back. He replaces my finger with his own and gently massages the front wall of my passage. I lift my head to look at him but as I do, his face disappears between my thighs and his tongue darts out to taste me.

"Oh!" I cry before dropping my head back onto the bed. He expertly circles that hot spot with his tongue, while pumping his finger back and forth inside me. I grab fist-fulls of the top sheet and my back reflexively arches. A loud cry rushes from deep inside me as I tumble rapidly towards climax. He increases the pace of his finger thrusts and flicks of his tongue and I writhe uncontrollably. His other hand clamps down on my stomach from under my thigh, so he's wrapped right around my leg. My other leg juts out in a spasm and lands on his shoulder. "Fuck!" I can't help screaming at the top of my lungs. This is all new to me.

Suddenly, he withdraws his finger and pulls away from me. He stands up and I gaze up at him with a deep frown. My pleasure cascading out of my body as swiftly as it had arrived. He's still rock hard and glistening in the fading, crimson light.

"By rights, I ought to leave you like that. It would serve you right. You desperately need more, yes?"

"Yes!" I gasp, half sitting up. "Please, I need more."

"That's how you left me earlier. It was most unpleasant."

"I'm sorry," I say, my voice breaking. "I won't do it again. It was supposed to pay you back for this morning."

"I know that," he says, his lip curling. He strokes his cock, still staring at my body. "But I'm the captain and I take my pleasure when I want it."

"Aye, Captain. I understand. Do you want it now?"

"I fucking do. That's the problem. I'm torn." He puts his knee on the bed between my spread thighs and flicks a finger over my swollen nub of ecstasy. "Maybe I'll torment you some more."

I groan and roll my eyes back, arching my back so my

breasts heave up towards his face. He dips his finger into me again and begins to stroke back and forth.

"Or perhaps I'll finish what you started in your mouth. Would you like that? If I come in your hot, wet mouth?"

I can't answer, all I can do is moan and writhe. Intense pleasure threatens to drown me completely. But I open my mouth as wide as it will go, inviting him in.

He releases me and moves up my body until he is kneeling either side of my shoulders. He drops his weight forward onto his outstretched arms and thrusts his cock into my waiting mouth. He wastes no time and thrusts his hips, pushing his cock to the back of my throat. I gag but hold myself together. I tip my head back so that he can reach deeper down my throat.

A moan rises from my chest and the vibration seems to spur him on. He pumps hard and fast. I can hardly breathe and I half-gag with every thrust. But damn, it feels incredible anyway. I clamp my hands onto his thighs and arch my back. But I miss his finger inside me. I reach down to take care of it myself, rubbing my finger against the sensitive nub. The surge is intense and glorious.

Jim grunts with his thrusts and I fear he may be close to finishing. But he pulls out of my mouth, leaving me gasping for breath. He moves quickly back down my body and lies on top of me, resting on his elbows as he strokes my face and hair.

"I want to pleasure you. I'm no brute."

"Well, thank you," I reply, unable to hide my grin.

He lifts his hips and uses his hand to guide himself into me. I wrap my legs around him and accept the full length of him into my slick, wet passage.

I capture his face in both of my hands and he kisses me softly, tenderly as he rocks his hips gently. My whole body tingles. The feel of him inside me is electrifying. His soft kiss only amplifies the sensation. His fingers stroke my hair and his chest crushes mine. He moves in me like that; long, languid strokes; until the room is completely dark. I couldn't describe it as fucking. It's so far from that. This is intense and emotional. Is this what lovemaking feels like? When my climax comes, it's deeper, more primal, than before. Tears come, unbidden as he brings me to the cusp of sanity. I am at the edge of a cliff and I fall. A cry comes out of my mouth that feels as though it belongs to someone else. I'm falling, falling, falling.

He swells in me, filling me even more fully than I think possible. His mouth is on my throat, kissing and licking the sweat from my skin. He comes hard, thrusting almost painfully into me. His cock pulses as his seed rushes up the length of it and spills inside me. I'm far too out of my mind to truly notice or care. All I can think is how incredible it feels. He is my world and I am his.

Slowly, wordlessly, he slows down his rocking until he is nestled deep inside me without moving. I open my eyes and look into his. He strokes my face and kisses my lips.

"Are you all right?"

"More than all right," I say with a chuckle. "You have to stay inside me forever. I won't let you go." I clamp my ankles behind him and grip him with my knees.

"I don't feel like that would be practical, I'm afraid. I can hardly captain my ship like this."

I burst out laughing and there, at the corner of his eyes and beneath his beard... a small smile!

"Fuck," he says softly, shaking his head. "Woman, you'll ruin me. I'm going soft."

"That is not something a woman wants to hear." I shake my head.

"Hmph," he grunts. "It's inevitable after a session like that." He pulls out of me and groans as he drops onto the bed beside me. "I'm getting too old for this."

His seed trickles out of me and I stare at his magnificent face beside me, still not quite caring about consequences. He takes my near hand and raises it to his lips.

There are words on the tip of my tongue. Not those words—not yet—but something close. Something dangerous. But fear rises, curling around my heart like smoke. This is temporary. It has to be. I can't afford to feel more than I should. And I won't say a thing—not tonight. Maybe not ever.

CHAPTER EIGHT

It's still dark when I wake. I'm lying with my back to Jim as his fingers trace gentle circles on my hip and I turn my face towards him. His eyes catch the faint starlight through the bay of windows.

"Go back to sleep," he whispers.

"If you wanted me to sleep, you shouldn't have woken me with this." I tap his hand, still caressing my hip.

"I apologise." He takes a deep breath. "No, I don't." He pulls me closer to him, pressing me against his naked body. He's hard again and it presses against my backside. He tucks his other arm under my head, wraps it around me and gently cups my breast in his hand. His lips kiss my shoulder.

I remove his hand from my breast and thread my fingers through his, but allow his wandering hand to explore my skin.

"I'm too tired."

"Understood."

I close my eyes and nestle myself against him. I really am too tired, but I like the feeling of his eagerness to be with me.

"I know almost nothing about you," I say softly into the dark cloaking us.

"What would you like to know?"

"You're very well spoken for a pirate. Where are you from?"

He clears his throat and moves his circling fingers to my thigh. "England."

"That's not very precise." A smile tugs at my lips.

"Well, my grandfather was the second son of a Lord. His elder brother inherited the title and lands, so he had to chart his own course. He bought a ship with what little money he had and started a trading business. Within two years he had three ships sailing around the Mediterranean. My father took over the business when my grandfather passed away. Unlike my grandfather, he was much more hands-on and would sail with his ships, seeking out the best trade deals and venturing into new routes and products. I spent my early years at sea with a governess and a hundred sailors. I was taught the family trade, which by this point had flourished into a very profitable one. I never lacked for anything. When we were at home—a large property in London—I attended a good school. But the sea called to me and when I left school I went straight back to work for my father. His navigator, a man named Elias Mercer, taught me everything there is to know about sailing. He taught me how to lead by example and that a good captain should know how to run his own ship, not just order better men to do all the work. So, yes, I'm well spoken because I come from aristocracy and attended Eton. But I am a man of the sea and in many ways, Mercer was more a father to me than my own. I owe him everything."

I listen to him talk about his life with quiet attention, caressing the back of his hand with my thumb.

"It sounds like he was a good mentor."

"The very best."

"What changed? Why did you turn to this life?"

His fingers go still and his breath quickens slightly. Silence draws out.

"It's difficult to talk about," he says at last.

"I understand. You can trust me, if you want to say more. But if not, that's all right." I squeeze his hand and wriggle against him for reassurance.

"I'll just say that my father did something unforgivable and I had no choice but to turn away from him."

There's nothing I can say to that, I simply hold the space for him.

After a while, I untuck my fingers from between his and guide his hand back to my breast, in hopes that my body can pull him back from the chasm I sense he's staring into. He gently begins to knead where I placed his hand and his lips whisper across the back of my shoulder. He pulls his hips back from my buttocks just enough to spring his erection loose from between us and he guides it between my thighs. I obligingly cock my leg as he slips it into me, then close my legs again to grip him tightly inside me. He returns his hand to my hip and holds it in place as he begins to rock slowly back and forth.

The way he fills me up is like nothing I've ever felt before and I honestly feel as though I will never be this satisfied again in my life. I need him inside me all the time.

We lay like that, gently rocking with the motion of the ship for what might be an hour or more. It's slow and sleepy and sensual. There's no enormous climax, just quiet satisfaction, which is exactly what we both need. His cock presses against the front of my inner passage, due to the angle and doesn't go as deep as in other positions. The head rubs back and forth and brings me to a low simmer. I murmur appreciatively to let him know that it feels good. He kisses my shoulder and neck and continues to squeeze my full breast. This might be heaven. I haven't quite decided.

His rocking slows and gradually stops, but he remains hard inside me. He just holds me close against his front and slides his left arm out from under me to prop his head up on his hand.

"I know almost nothing about you, either," he says, curiosity in his quiet voice.

"There's not much to know. I was born and raised in Charleston. My mother died when I was young. My father died when I was fifteen, so I had to fend for myself. I started working in a tavern like the one Briggs found me in. Six years later I find myself in bed with a pirate captain through sheer dumb luck."

"There must be more. You're more interesting than you make out."

I chuckle. "I don't think so."

"I find you fascinating. You're strong-willed and independent. Not like most young women your age."

"I've had to be." I shrug. "I had to get by and the world is cruel to young women. So I grew tough."

"True. Can I ask... I hate to... but I'm also insanely curious... you're so experienced."

"You want to know how many men I've been with?" I try not to laugh at his awkwardness.

"It's none of my business." He slowly resumes rocking and I catch my breath. "Let me just enjoy the feel of you."

"All right. But if you still want to know when you've finished, I'll tell you."

He grunts something unintelligible and forcefully rolls me onto my front without slipping out of me. He's on my back for a second before pulling himself up onto his knees and dragging me with him. I brace my hands under me and push up onto all fours. His fingers grasp my hips tightly, digging into the flesh and he starts pumping his hips back and forth with enthusiastic vigour. His cock rams into me hard and fast taking me right to the border between pleasure and pain. I whimper with every rapid thrust and surge after surge rushes through my body. My arms shake under me and I throw my head back with a huge cry as the biggest wave yet hits me.

"Fuck!" I yell. "Yes!"

He grunts along with his thrusts. Between both of our vocalisations and the wet, sloppy noises of his cock and my dripping wet cunt, this is by far the noisiest we've been since we started this affair.

"Fuuuuck!" he roars. His cock swells painfully inside me and he thrusts erratically as his cum surges into me. His groin smashes against mine, rocking me hard on my shaking arms. They collapse beneath me and I groan my way through the end of my climax, my face smooshed into the mattress. He presses his hands down hard on my buttocks and his hips jerk hard. I feel the head of his cock right up inside me, hammering against what feels like a brick wall. I whimper and writhe, trying to pull away. But he holds me fast as he finishes off. Finally he is still and his cock merely twitches inside me rather than thrusting, sending after shocks through me. I moan every curse word I know.

He pulls slowly out of me, still holding my hips up. I tug free, unable to stay in this position and fall onto my side. He drops onto the bed beside me.

"How many?" He demands.

I open my mouth to answer but he shakes his head.

"No. Don't tell me." He pulls me to him and I gasp as his seed gushes out of me. He kisses me deeply, his tongue probing inside my mouth. He pulls back and strokes my hair. "Give me half an hour and we'll do that again."

"Sounds good," I say, smiling drunkenly at him. I want to explode like that as often as possible and I decide I love the feel of him finishing in me. I've been missing out all this time. Although, if I'd allowed it to happen often, I'd have half a dozen babies by now and would never have found myself here.

"This is bliss," he says sleepily, his eyes drifting closed.

"Hmm," I murmur in reply. "You don't have anyone to talk to like this normally, do you?"

"No. I haven't been comfortable enough to open up with anyone for—" His eyes open, look at me and then close again with a sigh. "Over four years."

"You sound pretty confident about that time." I hold him tight, worried he might roll away. But he keeps equally tight hold of me and kisses my forehead.

"I am, yes."

He's not going to expand on it and I wonder if it's connected to whatever pulled him away from his family. I set my curiosity aside and snuggle against his hot body. We drift off to sleep in each others arms, the bedsheets a damp and twisted mess beneath our naked and sweaty bodies.

I wake abruptly some time later. Jim has untangled our limbs and sits upright on the bed, his head tilted to one side.

"Something's wrong," he says sharply.

"What?" I ask blearily, wiping sleep from my eyes. I notice it then. The ship is rocking more severely than usual. I'm alert in an instant and looking around the dark cabin. The hammock is swinging wildly but almost everything else in the cabin is secured and unmoving.

Above us, a bell suddenly rings out in the quiet, tolling fast.

Jim's eyes are bright and he leaps from the bed. "Storm."

CHAPTER NINE

The sharp clang of the warning bell shatters the stillness of the cabin, sending a jolt through me. Jim curses under his breath, hastily tugging his shirt over his head while I scramble to fasten the laces of my bodice. The ship gives a sudden lurch, the tell-tale groan of straining wood reverberating through the walls.

I stagger after him into his study, only half dressed. I barely have time to steady myself before Jim is shrugging into his coat, his face already hardened into the sharp mask of command. The warmth I felt from him moments ago is gone, replaced with the cold efficiency of a man who has spent years steering men through tempests.

"Stay here," he orders, strapping on his belt and reaching for his hat. "I mean it, Hester. This storm's coming fast, and I don't have time to be looking over my shoulder for you."

I yank on my boots, ignoring the way my fingers tremble as I fasten them. "I can help."

"You'll help by staying out of the way." His gaze flickers to me, dark and intense, there's no softness in it now—only the clipped authority of a captain. "Lock the door if it gets bad."

A gust of wind howls through the ship as another violent tilt sends the lantern swinging wildly on its hook. The warning bell rings again, more frantic this time. Jim swears, crossing to the door and throwing it open, revealing a deck already slick with rain and chaos. The air is thick with salt and panic.

I clench my jaw. "I'm not hiding in here while the rest of you fight to keep this ship afloat."

Jim turns back, his expression thunderous. "Hester—"

"No." I step forward, lifting my chin. "I will not cower below while men are risking their lives. If I can help, I will."

For a second, neither of us speaks, the storm raging louder outside. Then, with a low growl of frustration, Jim grabs my wrist and drags me to him, his lips crashing against mine in a kiss that is rough, desperate, and far too brief.

He pulls away, his forehead resting against mine for the barest of moments. "Stay close to me. Don't do anything reckless."

Then he is gone, striding onto the deck, already barking orders to his crew. I swallow hard, steeling myself, before following him into the storm.

The moment I emerge, the wind slams into me like a living force, stealing my breath. Rain lashes against my skin in sharp, stinging bursts, soaking through my clothes in an instant. The ship heaves beneath my feet, the deck drenched with seawater and the churn of the storm. Above, the sails snap and the masts groan under the strain, ropes creaking as the rigging fights against the wind's fury.

Men scramble to their positions, hauling on lines, securing barrels, and battling to keep the ship upright as towering waves crash against the hull. The air is thick with shouted orders, the thud of boots against wood, and the ever-present roar of the sea.

Jim stands near the helm, gripping the rail as he shouts commands over the storm. Lightning flashes, illuminating his profile—his jaw set, his coat whipping around him as he braces against the gale. Even in the chaos, his presence commands the crew, each man moving with urgency under his orders.

I grip the nearest railing, steadying myself as I make my way toward him, my boots slipping on the wet wood. A hand grabs my arm, yanking me back before I can take another step. I turn, heart hammering, to find Briggs glowering at me.

"Are you mad?" he shouts over the storm. "You'll get yourself killed!"

"I can help!" I shout back, shaking off his grip.

A massive wave slams against the side of the ship, sending a rush of seawater over the deck. I gasp as it drenches me, nearly knocking me off my feet. Briggs curses, grabbing onto the nearest rope to keep himself upright. I manage to catch hold of a barrel, my nails digging into the wet wood.

Jim's voice cuts through the storm. "Hester! Get below!"

I look up to see him staring at me, his face taut with frustration and worry. Another flash of lightning ignites the sky behind him, turning him into a stark silhouette against the storm.

I shake my head, wiping the water from my eyes. "I won't hide!"

He mutters a curse, but there's no time to argue. The ship tilts hard, and timbers creak with the strain. A cry goes up from the rigging—one of the men is struggling with a loose line, the rope whipping dangerously in the wind. Without thinking, I push forward, gripping the nearest post for balance as I make my way toward the struggling sailor.

Jim sees me moving and shouts something I can't hear over the storm, but I don't stop. If I can keep my footing, I can help. If I can just—

A wave crashes over the deck, surging around my ankles, but I dig my heels in and push forward. The wind tears at me, my soaked skirts clinging to my legs, but I force myself to keep moving. The sailor is gripping the flailing rope, his knuckles white, his feet slipping dangerously as he fights to gain control.

I throw myself forward, seizing the rope just as another gust threatens to rip it from his grasp. The coarse fibres bite into my palms, but I hold on, bracing myself against the deck. "Pull!" I shout, my voice barely carrying over the storm.

Together, we drag the rope taut, securing it around a cleat as the ship bucks beneath us. The sailor pants, nodding his thanks before rushing off to help another struggling crew mate. I take a shaky breath, the adrenaline thrumming through my veins, but there's no time to rest. Another shout rises above the storm—a man struggling to drag a half-barrel of supplies back toward the hatch before it tumbles into the sea. The ship lurches, and the barrel crashes against the deck, knocking the sailor off balance.

I push forward without thinking, grabbing the other side of the heavy barrel. The sailor looks up, startled, but then nods, bracing himself as we both heave against the weight. Rain pours over us in relentless sheets, making the deck slippery beneath our boots, but inch by inch, we wrestle the barrel toward safety. My muscles burn with effort, but I grit my teeth and push through.

With a final shove, we get the barrel to the hatch, securing it before the next wave can send it overboard. The sailor grips my arm briefly in thanks before rushing off to another task. My breath comes in ragged gasps, my limbs shaking from exertion, but I force myself to straighten. The storm isn't done yet, and neither am I.

A sudden crack of wood above makes me snap my head up. The wind howls through the rigging, and I barely have time to register what's happening before a loose spar, torn free from the mast, comes hurtling toward the deck. The men scatter, ducking away from its path, but I'm caught in the chaos, my boots slipping on the wet planks as I try to move.

A flash of fear grips me as the spar crashes down, the heavy wood splintering as it strikes the deck mere feet from where I stand. I stagger, my balance failing as the ship tilts sharply, the force sending me careening toward the rail.

A strong arm seizes me just as my feet leave the deck. I gasp, the world tilting wildly as I'm yanked back from the brink and pulled hard against a solid chest. Jim's grip is iron, his arm wrapped tight around my waist as he hauls me away from danger. His breath is ragged, his pulse pounding beneath my hand where I clutch his damp shirt.

"Bloody hell, Hester!" His voice is raw, filled with frustration and something dangerously close to fear. "I told you to stay below!"

I'm shaking too hard to respond, my heart hammering as I try to catch my breath. The spar lies shattered where I would have been, the deck littered with debris and seawater. Jim's hold on me doesn't loosen, his fingers digging into my side as he steadies us both against the ship's wild motion.

"You could have been killed!" he snarls, his face inches from mine, rain dripping from his hair, his jaw clenched tight.

"So could all of you!" I shoot back, finding my voice despite the way my body trembles. "I won't stand by and do nothing."

His grip tightens for a moment, a muscle twitching in his jaw. His crew is still scrambling around him, men shouting orders, but his focus is locked on me. His thumb brushes my hip, whether to reassure himself I'm still there or to restrain me, I can't tell.

Then, with a sharp breath, he releases me. "Fine," he bites out, his voice low and rough. "But if you're staying, you stay near me. Understand?"

I nod, unable to form words. His gaze lingers, storm-dark

and intense, before he turns sharply, barking more orders to his men. I shake off my fear, steady my footing, and follow him back into the fray.

Through the rest of the storm, I shadow Jim's every step, watching as he commands his crew with precision honed from years at sea. He moves with the confidence of a man who has weathered worse, barking orders that cut through the howling wind, his grip steady on the wheel when he takes it, guiding The Stormchaser through the worst of the gale. I catch glimpses of him in flashes of lightning—his jaw clenched, his coat plastered to his body by the rain, his hands never wavering despite the storm's fury.

The night feels endless, a battle fought against the elements with nothing but skill and willpower to keep us afloat. The wind screams around us, the waves hammer the hull, but the crew fights on, hauling ropes, tightening sails, doing everything in their power to keep the ship from breaking apart beneath us. Every muscle in my body aches, exhaustion settling deep into my bones, but I don't stop. I can't stop. I'm right there in the thick of it, hauling on ropes and adding my weight to the wheel to turn the ship against the raging wind and sea.

Then, as if the storm itself has grown weary, the wind begins to ease. The rain softens from a relentless assault to a wind-whipped drizzle. The first light of dawn creeps over the horizon, casting a pale glow over the battered deck. The sea, though still restless, no longer threatens to swallow us whole. The Stormchaser has survived.

The crew, drenched and spent, begin to slump where they stand, leaning against the railings, dropping to sit wherever they can. Some laugh weakly, shaking their heads at the sheer madness of the night, while others simply close their eyes, breathing deep, ragged sighs of relief. The ship creaks beneath us, groaning from the strain it has endured, but it still floats, still sails.

Jim stands at the helm, his hands braced on the wheel, staring out at the horizon as if daring the sea to challenge him again. He looks utterly exhausted, his shoulders sagging for the first time since the bell rang. I step toward him, feeling the ache in my limbs with every movement.

He turns his head slightly, his eyes finding mine. For a long moment, we just look at each other. The tension of the night lingers between us, unspoken but understood. Then, slowly, he exhales.

"Go back to my cabin. I'll be there shortly." There's quiet fury in his voice. A dark and dangerous edge that unnerves me. I nod meekly and make my way carefully over the slippery deck, down the steep steps and into his quarters.

I reach the bedroom and peel off my sopping wet clothes. I stand before the wash basin, shaking and covered in goosebumps. I slowly wash myself with what remains of the soapy water. Some of it has spilled in the tumult. Still naked, I mop the floor in front of the basin and where my wet clothes have left a puddle on the floor. I bundle the clothes into the hamper next to the hammock and resolve to do all of the laundry later today.

The door bangs open and a drenched Jim strides towards me.

"Why are you so angry?" I ask, flinching from him. His eyes blaze but his rage doesn't stop him from ogling my body. I don't even attempt to cover myself. I lean on the mop and plant my other hand on my hip.

"Because you made my job harder. I am responsible for those men!" He thrusts a finger towards the door. "Instead of being focused on them, I had to worry about you."

"I took care of myself."

"Until you didn't. Until you nearly went overboard. I was terrified, Hester! I thought I was going to lose you."

Heat rises in my cheeks.

"I'm sorry. I don't want to distract you. I just wanted to be of use."

He closes the gap between us, ripping off his coat as he does. He grabs me roughly and pushes my back up against the pillar that the hammock is attached to. His mouth crashes onto mine, hungry and desperate. And angry. I whimper in pain, his hands gripping my upper arms too tightly. He ignores my complaint and continues to thrash at my tongue with his.

This man's appetite is as insatiable as any man I've known. He pulls out of the kiss and shakes me by my arms.

"I need you to understand that when I give an order, I expect it to be followed."

"I do! Please, stop. I don't want to be with you while you're like this!" I cry out, tears spilling down my cheeks. He releases my arms and pushes me away. I stumble backwards into the hammock, my hands grabbing hold of the swinging rope to steady myself. I turn my head to look at him. He turns away from me.

"I'm furious, Hester." His voice is low now as he paces the room. "You put people in danger. But damn you—I want you too. You've bewitched me. I can't tell up from down any more. How can I be so angry and so full of desire all at once? This is why most sailors say that it's bad luck to have a woman aboard."

"I haven't done anything to you." I let go of the hammock and steady myself against the wooden pillar as the ship continues to rock. "You can't blame me for your lust. I'm just here." I am painfully aware that I am also naked, which somewhat weakens my point.

His head whips towards me and he fixes his blazing eyes on me.

"I've never felt like this before," he says, his voice rising again and something besides anger flickers across his face. Helplessness.

"Neither have I." I cross my arms over my chest. "But you don't have to worry about me being a distraction. You'll be rid of me as soon as we reach Nassau." I look away, tears still swimming in my eyes.

"Right," he says, nodding. "You'll be on the next ship home and I can go about my business. We never have to see each other again."

"Exactly." My chest aches and I let out a shaking breath.

"Depending on what that storm has done to our position, which I'm about to figure out, we should only be three days away now. Including the job we have to do."

I nod and wipe my face with my hands.

"I can go back to my bunk for the rest of the journey. I don't think the men are going to bother me now."

"That's probably for the best." His voice is cold and hard. He scoops up his wet jacket and leaves the room. I drop to the floor and clutch my knees to my chest as renewed sobs burst from me.

CHAPTER TEN

After dressing in clean clothes, I retrieve all my wet and otherwise soiled clothes from the hamper. The salt stiffening the storm-soaked fabric. I head down to the galley and descend even deeper into the ship to find a barrel of seawater with some shirts hanging to dry nearby. I set about washing my clothes. The water is frigid, but I hardly feel it. My movements are mechanical, my thoughts distant, my mind caught in the echo of Jim's words.

You put people in danger.

The accusation burns hotter than the sting of salt in the rope burns on my hands. I know he was worried, that his anger was fuelled by fear, but it does little to soften the ache his words left behind. I had only wanted to help. To prove that I wasn't a burden. And yet, in the end, I had only made things worse in his eyes.

The ship is quieter now, save for the groans of wood settling after the storm's rage. The men are too busy assessing the damage, repairing sails, and checking the hull for leaks to pay me any mind. Even Jim, who had been so quick to chastise me, has given me nothing more than a passing glance before throwing himself back into his duties.

I spend the day in a daze, my body weary, my mind clouded. I eat only when I remember to, my appetite dulled by exhaustion and the lingering sting of disappointment. I don't know what I expected from him—comfort, perhaps? A word of reassurance? Instead, I am met with indifference.

I remove all of my things from the captain's quarters and retreat to my solitary bunk in the corridor. I tuck my bag away under the bunk before heading to the galley to help serve dinner.

Night falls slowly, the ship rocking gently on calmer waters. After the men have eaten their fill, I return to my cramped bunk, the space too small, the mattress too thin to offer any real comfort. But I am too exhausted to care. I close my eyes, willing sleep to come quickly, to sweep me away from my thoughts.

But something keeps me awake.

A prickling sensation at the back of my neck. A weight that settles over my skin, unseen but undeniable.

Someone is watching me.

The next day, the sea is eerily calm, a stark contrast to the storm we barely survived. The tropical heat bears down on us, the air heavy and damp, making every movement sluggish despite the tension thickening the atmosphere. The crew moves with a quiet urgency, sweat gleaming on their brows as the lookout calls from above. "Sails ahead! It's the Sea Devil!"

A ripple of anticipation spreads across the deck. I hurry to the rail, gripping the worn wood as I strain my eyes toward the horizon. There, cutting through the waves, is a dark shape—a brigantine, its sails full, its flag unmistakable. The Sea Devil.

Jim stands at the helm, his gaze locked on the ship we've been chasing down for days, his face unreadable. "All hands to battle stations!" he calls, and the crew springs into action. Muskets are checked, blades sharpened, ropes coiled and ready. The Stormchaser surges forward, closing the distance with practised precision.

As the two ships draw alongside each other, the tension thickens. The Sea Devil's crew are already armed, lining the rails, their captain—a tall man with a cruel smirk—watching from the quarterdeck.

Jim raises a hand, and in an instant, the first shot rings out. Chaos erupts. Grappling hooks are thrown, ropes lash across the gap, and then the boarding begins. Jim is the first to leap, his cutlass flashing as he lands among the Sea Devil's men. His crew follows, spilling onto the Sea Devil in a clash of steel and gunfire.

I grip the rail, my knuckles white, my heart hammering in my chest. The deck of the Sea Devil is a blur of movement—men clashing, shouting, fighting for their lives. I scan the chaos, searching for Jim, but he is lost in the fray.

Then, through the smoke and struggle, I see Briggs and another crewman vanish below deck. I have no idea what they're after or why this battle is happening at all. No one has told me anything.

Minutes stretch into eternity. My breath quickens as I watch the battle rage, helpless to stop it. The Sea Devil lurches with the weight of men locked in combat. Muskets fire, blades flash, bodies fall.

And then—movement on our own deck. I hear the clatter of boots, the scrape of metal against wood, and turn just in time to see them.

Men from the Sea Devil have boarded The Stormchaser.

My stomach turns to ice. I stagger back from the rail, my breath catching in my throat. They're here, moving fast, weapons drawn. The crew left behind to guard the ship is caught off guard, scrambling to fight them off, but the enemy has the advantage. I need to move—I need to hide.

I turn and run.

My heart pounds as I weave through the chaos, dodging men, barrels, and the swinging of blades. My skirts snag on something, and I nearly fall, catching myself against a stack of crates. I can hear them behind me, their heavy steps, their curses. I don't stop. I sprint toward the galley, knowing there are places to hide there, but just as I round the corner, a hand snatches at my arm.

I twist, trying to break free, but the grip tightens. A pirate with wild, dirty hair and a cruel smile sneers down at me, his breath reeking of rum. "Where do you think you're going, pretty thing?" he growls.

Panic surges through me. I kick, claw, twist, anything to get away. He laughs, dragging me back toward the deck. I scream, but my voice is lost in the roar of the fight. No one hears me. No one is coming.

And then, suddenly, my captor stumbles forward with a grunt of pain. I wrench free, gasping, and turn to see young Ben standing there, a broken oar gripped in his hands, his face pale but determined.

"Run!" he shouts, swinging again.

I don't hesitate. I bolt for the nearest doorway, my heart hammering as the fight continues behind me. Ben holds his ground, the boy who once tormented me now my only protector.

I stumble through the narrow passage below deck, my breath coming in short gasps as I shove open the door to the storeroom. The scent of salt, wood, and damp provisions surrounds me as I press myself into the shadows between crates of supplies. The door creaks as it swings back into place, plunging me into darkness.

Above me, the sounds of battle rage on. The stomp of boots, the clash of steel, the crack of gunfire. The ship tilts sharply, sending barrels rattling in their braces, and I clamp a hand over my mouth to keep from crying out.

Muffled voices echo from the corridor outside. I strain to listen, my heart hammering in my chest. The voices are close—too close. Heavy footsteps pause just beyond the storeroom door.

I hold my breath, willing myself to disappear into the shadows as the latch rattles. The door shifts an inch, then stops. A rough laugh drifts through the thin wood, followed by a muttered curse before the boots retreat back toward the chaos above.

I release a shaky breath, my fingers still digging into the soft flesh of my cheek. The fight isn't over yet. And I'm not safe.

Time stretches in the darkness. My breath evens out, but my pulse remains rapid, ears straining to catch any hint of what's happening above. The clash of steel grows sporadic, the heavy footsteps less frantic. The shouting dulls, replaced by low voices, the occasional thud of something heavy being moved. Then, a different sensation entirely—the ship shifts beneath me, not in a chaotic battle surge, but a deliberate turn.

We're moving.

I push myself up slowly, hands shaking as I reach for the door. Pressing my ear against the wood, I listen. The tension in the air has changed. The violence has faded, but whether we've won or lost, I cannot tell. Swallowing hard, I gather my courage and ease the door open.

The corridor is empty, but the scent of blood lingers in the humid air. My footsteps are cautious as I make my way toward the hatch leading above deck. I hesitate before climbing the steps, my fingers gripping the rail as I brace myself for what I might find.

The deck is a mess—ropes scattered, bodies slumped, some groaning in pain, others eerily still. The Sea Devil is now nothing more than a dark shadow falling behind us, its sails in tatters. I don't know what happened, only that The Stormchaser is moving away, the tension thick but no longer crackling with battle energy.

I scan the deck for Jim, but my eyes catch Ben first. He's slumped against a crate, breathing hard, a cut above his brow leaking blood down his cheek. Our eyes meet, and something unspoken passes between us. Gratitude. Recognition. I nod at him, and he gives me a weak, lopsided smile before tipping his head back against the crate, spent.

I move carefully across the deck, stepping over discarded weapons and sidestepping the men tending to the wounded. The tropical heat presses down on me, thick and suffocating, amplifying the smell of blood and sweat. I still don't know if we've won or lost, only that we are leaving the Sea Devil behind.

The captain's quarters loom ahead, the door closed, an imposing barrier between me and whatever answers lie beyond. I hesitate, my fingers hovering just above the handle. After everything, I don't know if I'll be welcome inside.

Before I can turn the handle, the door is flung open. I startle, taking a step back as Briggs nearly collides with me. He halts abruptly, his eyes widening in surprise. His gaze flicks over his shoulder, hesitating as if waiting for instruction.

A rough voice from within—Jim's—breaks the silence. "Let her in."

Briggs exhales sharply, then steps aside, allowing me to enter. I move past him cautiously, my gaze sweeping over the cabin. The scent of sweat, gunpowder, and salt lingers in the air, mixing with the faint aroma of rum. The room is dim, lit only by the lantern swaying from the ceiling, casting flickering light across the space.

At the captain's table, slumped in a chair, is a man I do not recognize. His face is lined with exhaustion, his skin pale beneath the grime and bruises. His clothes hang loose on his frame, torn and stained, and one of his wrists is wrapped in a bloodied bandage. His eyes, sharp despite his obvious weakness, flicker to me as I step forward. It's hard to gauge his age, given his rough state, but he looks older than the captain.

Jim stands nearby, arms crossed, his expression unreadable. "Hester," he says, his voice rough with exhaustion. "This is Elias Mercer."

The name strikes a chord, echoing back to a conversation we had in his bed. Jim had spoken of him before—his father's old navigator, the man he owed everything to.

Jim sets his dark eyes on me. "Our pursuit of the Sea Devil was a rescue mission. We succeeded."

CHAPTER ELEVEN

Briggs gives a curt nod before leaving and shutting the door behind him with a quiet click. His absence leaves a charged silence in the room, the dim lantern light casting flickering shadows along the walls. Jim's eyes find mine almost instantly, scanning my face, taking in every loose hair, every smudge of grime left from the battle.

"Are you hurt?" His voice is low, gruff with exhaustion.

I shake my head. "I'm fine."

His gaze lingers a moment longer, as if searching for any sign of weakness I might not admit to. When he seems satisfied, he exhales sharply and turns back toward the table where Elias Mercer sits slumped, his fingers tracing the edges of a map spread before him.

I step forward, my curiosity outweighing my hesitation. Jim takes a seat at the table and gestures to an empty chair, and I sink into it, my fingers ghosting over the rough parchment. The markings are unlike anything I've ever seen—columns of numbers, strange symbols scattered across the page, and a winding series of lines that seem to form no clear route.

"What is this?" I ask, glancing between them.

"What I was captured for," Elias says, his voice gruff.

Jim pours three glasses of rum and passes one to me. I take it, eager to have something to take away the remaining edge of fear leftover from the battle. I examine the map, running a finger over one of the columns of numbers near the edge.

"It's not a normal map."

Elias shakes his head slowly, his voice hoarse when he speaks. "It's a coded map. It'll lead us to untraceable gold that the Spanish never want to be found."

Jim leans forward, his forearms resting against the edge of the table. "And you're the only one who can read it."

Elias chuckles dryly, though the sound turns into a cough. "Aye. And that's why Kane kept me alive."

A shiver runs through me, but I force myself to focus. This map was worth taking a man captive for, worth Jim risking his crew to retrieve. And now, it's in our hands.

"So where does it lead?" I ask, bracing myself for the answer.

Elias exchanges a glance with Jim before dragging a finger along one of the lines. "That's the question, isn't it?" He takes a deep drink and smacks his thin lips.

He exhales slowly, eyes flicking over the strange markings as if reacquainting himself with an old secret. He traces a calloused finger over one of the columns of numbers, muttering under his breath before he nods to himself.

"Aye," he says at last. "This here—these coordinates—they point to an island. Small. Barely worth a mark on any map, but I know it's there."

Jim's brows pull together in concentration. "Where?"

Elias takes another slow sip of his drink, savouring it before setting the glass down with a dull clink. "Just north-west of Nassau. No more than a day's sail with fair winds."

Jim shifts in his chair, fingers tapping against the table. "Have you been there already?"

Elias smirks, though there's little humour in it. "Aye, lad. I've seen the treasure myself. But without a ship to move it, so I left it behind and came looking for you. Kane found me first."

Jim glances down at the map, studying the markings as if he can will them into making sense. "You're certain Kane doesn't know where to go?"

"As certain as I can be." Elias leans back, his exhaustion visible in every movement. "He would've gutted me if I'd told him, but he still wouldn't have found it. You hit him hard. He won't be going anywhere until he repairs his ship."

Jim nods. "Then rest while you can. I'll tell the helmsman to set course for Nassau. When we get closer, you can guide us to the right island."

Elias doesn't argue. He drains the last of his drink and leans back in his chair, eyes already heavy with exhaustion. Jim looks to me, his expression unreadable.

"You should rest too," he says.

But I'm not certain I'll be able to sleep—not with the weight of this discovery pressing down on me.

Jim pushes back his chair with a scrape of wood against wood, his movements brisk and efficient despite the fatigue etched into his face. He drains the last of his rum in one swallow and straightens, rolling his shoulders as if shaking off the weight of the past few hours.

"I'll see to the course," he says, more to Elias than to me.

Elias grunts in acknowledgement, already half-slumped in his chair, rubbing at his bandaged wrist. Jim casts one last glance in my direction—his eyes lingering, unreadable—before striding to the door and pulling it open. The dim lantern light catches on the sharp lines of his profile for a moment, and then he is gone, the door clicking shut behind him.

Silence settles between Elias and me, heavy but not quite uncomfortable. He watches me, eyes sharp despite his weariness, studying me the way a man studies an unfamiliar chart—assessing, searching for meaning in the details.

He huffs out a soft chuckle, shaking his head. “So,” he says at last. “Who in blazes are you?”

I blink, caught off guard. “Hester,” I answer hesitantly.

“No surname?” His lips quirk, but there’s something shrewd in his gaze, something that makes me feel exposed.

I hesitate, then lift my chin. “Hester Rhodes.”

Elias nods as if filing the name away. “And how did a lass like you end up on The Stormchaser?”

I shift under his scrutiny. “By mistake, mostly.”

He snorts. “Jim doesn’t take on passengers by mistake.”

I say nothing. I don’t know what Jim tells his men about me. Maybe he doesn’t mention me at all.

Elias watches me for a long moment, then leans back, rubbing a hand over his jaw. “There’s something between you two. I can see it plain as day.”

My breath catches, but I force my expression to remain neutral. “That’s not—”

He holds up a hand, stopping me mid-sentence. “Don’t bother denying it, lass. I may be half-dead, but I’m not blind. Jim’s always been a hard man to read, but I know that look. Seen it before.”

I frown. “What look?”

Elias just smiles knowingly and takes another slow sip of his drink. “You’ll figure it out.”

I cast him a curious glance before knocking back the rest of my rum.

“Well, I’d love to pick your memories of a young Jim

Blackthorne, but I'd best leave you to rest." I get up from the table and head out onto the deck. I glance up to see Jim talking with his helmsman and go on my way, back to my meagre bunk. I collapse onto it and sleep claims me swiftly, despite the doors banging and men shouting and the general hubbub of the ship and its crew.

"Dinner!" A sharp voice cuts into my sleep, along with a nudge to my leg. I open my eyes and see Cook glaring down at me. I climb out of the small bunk and follow him up the corridor to the galley, wiping the sleep from my eyes.

"This is for the captain," Cook says, pointing a stubby finger towards a bubbling soup. "There's bread too." He returns to the thin broth for the rest of the men.

I check the cupboard and find half a loaf of bread. I cut the stale end off it and slice the rest to serve with the soup. I pour the soup into a large dish and stack the bread up beside it on a platter. With a heavy heart at the thought of returning to the cabin that previously held such positive associations, I carry the platter carefully up through the narrow corridors and out onto the deck. Night has fallen and lanterns swing to the rocking of the ship. I make my way across the deck to the captain's door and knock against it with my foot.

"Come in," Jim calls, though his voice is subdued. I look at the door and my full hands and heave a sigh.

"I have my hands full," I call through the door. A chair scrapes and a low chuckle meets my ears. The door opens and Jim stands there with his shirt half undone. Elias is at the table and there are two empty bottles of rum in front of him. I press my lips together and try not to look into Jim's bearded face. "Dinner is served."

He stands aside, swaying slightly. I enter the room and place the platter on the table as the door clicks shut behind me.

"It's mushroom," I say, laying out bowls and spoons. "There's no butter for the bread, but it should be fine dunked in the soup."

Jim drops into his chair at the head of the table and clears his throat.

"The rum's gone."

"Point me in the right direction," Elias says, his speech slurred. "And I'll get some more."

"I'll fetch some," I say, trying not to lose patience. I feel Jim's gaze on me as I turn away from the table and a throaty laugh follows me that I know can't belong to the brooding captain. I leave the cabin and pause for a moment once I close the door.

"No idea how you keep your hands off her," Elias says, still chuckling.

"It's fucking hard, I tell you." Jim's voice cuts like a knife.

I draw a sharp breath and push away from the door. Darkness clings to the deck with deep shadows bobbing with the sway of the lanterns. I cross the deck and go below the bow. I pass the galley and enter the storeroom. I light a lantern hanging from a hook by the door and lift it off the hook. Beside the door is a hatch in the floor. I hoist it open and hook it back against the wall. Carefully, I lower myself onto the ladder and step cautiously into the pitch black, the lantern in my tight grip.

I step off the ladder into a narrow store deep in the belly of the ship. Along the wall to my left is a rack filled with bottles of wine, rum and mead. Beside the ladder is a barrel of beer that drips steadily onto the floor from the tap. The tangy smell fills my nostrils and my boots track the sticky residue with them as I cross to the rack. I look for a bottle of rum among the many bottles, though around a third of the spaces are empty after nearly a week at sea. I find what I'm looking for and lift the bottle off the rack.

Movement catches my eye and I turn, shining the lantern towards the hatch. A pair of feet drop down onto the first rung. My chest tightens as the man descends, huffing and wheezing slightly. I cling to the lantern and rum bottle.

"Who goes there?" I ask, my voice small in the compact space.

The figure steps down from the ladder and turns towards me. Briggs faces me, stinking of beer and leering at me unpleasantly.

"Just me, lass," he says, swaying.

"Right. Well, I'll get out of your way." I move to pass him but he leans across my path, planting his hand on the wall beside the ladder.

"Now, now, there's no rush." He sucks a breath between his teeth. The lantern casts eerie shadows across his face. "What is it about you, eh?"

"What do you mean?"

"The Cap'n has been... not himself since he's been dipping his quill in your ink well. You put a spell on him? You a siren in our midst?"

"What? No." I step back. My heart beats a furious rhythm.

"It's not as if he's a stranger to womanly charms. Different whore in every port for the last few years. Ever since—well, anyway. But you're different. You got him all twisted in knots. What's so magical about your cunt, eh?"

A jolt of fear spikes through me, and I press myself against the rack of bottles.

"Have to try it for me'self. See if you do the same to me." He staggers towards me, dropping his breeches.

"I don't think so." I say, clutching the rum against my chest. He reaches for me and grabs a fistful of my hair.

"On your knees and open your mouth, lass. Best not struggle too much."

CHAPTER TWELVE

Briggs pushes down on my head but I twist under his arm and shove him away clumsily, my hands full. His eyes pop wide and he swings his hand out of the darkness, slapping me hard across the cheek with a crack. Shock paralyses me. My body shakes and my cheek throbs.

He pushes me back and the bottles clink behind me. “Stop the high ‘n’ mighty act, whore. You took gold to service my men. Now do your fucking job.”

Briggs lunges for me and I side-step him. I lift the rum bottle and bring it down on the top of his head. The glass shatters and rum spills down his face. He roars as shards of glass rain down onto the sticky floor. Still clutching the broken bottle neck and the lantern, I thrust the sharp edge of glass into his raised forearm, drawing blood. He cries and staggers backwards, bumping into the wall. I run past him and climb the ladder, my foot slipping on the second rung and my hands next to useless. I daren’t let go of anything and struggle up the ladder while he shouts and curses behind me. His hand reaches out and grabs the back of my dress. I let out a cry and tear free of him, my dress ripping and leaving him staggering away from the ladder.

I climb out of the hatch and stumble out of the storeroom and along the corridor. I pass the galley, which is packed with men. Tears stream down my face but I don't stop, don't make a sound until I feel fresh air on my face. I rush out onto the deck. The moon hangs low in the sky, shining silver on the tarred wood.

"Help!" I cry as I charge between cargo crates. "Jim!" I run, half limping right to his door and burst through it without knocking. He's on his feet and half way to the door, his face full of concern.

"What happened?" he asks, closing the gap between us and quickly scanning me with his dark eyes. Elias gets to his feet too, observing me with narrowed eyes.

"Briggs," I gasp, panting for breath. "He attacked me in the storeroom." I hold up the bottle neck, blood glistening on the jagged edge. The lantern is hot in my hand and suddenly I remember it's there. I wince and almost drop it, but Jim catches it and sets it on his desk.

"Attacked you? Tell me exactly what happened." His voice is too calm. Doesn't he understand?

"I was fetching you more rum and he came down the ladder behind me. He told me to get on my knees and earn my coin. He grabbed my hair." I point to where he pulled on it and Jim examines my scalp, sucking air between his teeth. Am I bleeding? "I pushed him off and he slapped me." I raise my fingers to my cheek, which throbs painfully.

"I see," Jim says, his voice low and threatening.

"I hit him over the head with the bottle." I hold up the broken neck and Jim gently pries it from my tight grip, also setting it aside. My hand aches from holding it so tightly. Both hands now empty begin to shake. My legs follow suit and I collapse to the floor. Jim squats in front of me, now utterly sober as he continues to look me over. He finds the back of my dress torn and a low growl rumbles from his chest.

He stands abruptly and grabs his belt where it hangs by the door. He unsheathes his cutlass and flings the door wide, storming out through it with a thunderous roar.

"Briggs! Where are you, you devil?!"

Elias helps me to my feet and holds onto me as we follow the captain onto the deck. Men turn and stare at us.

"Someone find the bastard and restrain him for me." Jim marches across the deck towards the door to the galley, his cutlass swinging wide of his body. Before he reaches it, it swings open, banging back against the wall. Briggs staggers out, his arm and head bleeding and covered in rum.

"There she is!" Briggs roars, pointing at me. "She attacked me!"

Men appear on either side of him and grab hold of his arms, holding him steady as the captain approaches. Elias and I follow but don't get too close. A circle of men forms around us, with more spilling out from wherever they've all been hiding.

"The way she tells it," the captain says, loud enough for all to hear. "You attacked her. She was defending herself."

"I'm injured, look!" Briggs says, holding up his bleeding right arm.

"I was very clear, Briggs. That first night when you tried to have my men use her in the most cruel and foul fashion, I was explicit about what would happen. Wasn't I?"

"I didn't do nothin', Cap'n." Briggs protests, struggling against the men holding him.

"You didn't try to force yourself on her? Didn't pull out her hair, slap her face, or rip her dress? None of these actions ringing a bell?" Jim barks, spittle flying. The men's gazes swing from the captain, to Briggs, to me. Heat rises in my cheeks. My hands are still shaking. Elias holds me firmly, his arm around my shoulders.

“You’d believe a dirty whore over your First Mate?” Briggs looks genuinely shocked.

Jim swiftly tosses his cutlass from his right hand to his left, catching it deftly. In one fluid movement, he launches his now empty fist at Briggs and punches him in the face with a sickening crunch. Blood gushes from Briggs’ nose and he collapses backwards with a whimper, held up only by his captors.

“Bring him over here.” Jim marches over to a stack of crates. He pulls one away from the rest. “Fetch rope.” The men follow his orders without question. Fear in every eye. Briggs is planted on his knees in front of the lone crate.

“No! No, I’m beggin’ you!” Briggs struggles but the other men are stronger.

Jim points from the rope in one man’s hands to the crate.

“Tie his arm down. The right one.”

“No!” Briggs yells, thrashing out.

I lift my hands to my face and cover my nose and mouth. My eyes are wide with horror, but I can’t look away. Fresh tears spill down my cheeks as Briggs is tied to the crate. The rope just below his elbow is tied especially tight, making his tanned skin turn white.

“You knew what would happen!” Jim shouts, leaning right into Briggs’ face. “You’re making me do this. Someone give up your belt.”

I don’t even see where it comes from, but a leather belt is slapped into Jim’s outstretched palm. He thrusts it between Briggs’ bared teeth. “Bite down on this,” Jim orders his First Mate.

Briggs bites into the leather, tears stain his face and he moans against the leather.

Without dragging it out, the captain raises his cutlass and

brings it down on Briggs' arm with a crunch of snapping bone. Blood gushes over the crate. Briggs screams against the belt. He falls backwards onto the deck. Every eye is on him.

"I was very clear," Jim says, his voice low but every man can hear him. We could hear a pin drop. "If any man lays a hand on Hester, he loses that hand. Crystal clear. I'm a man of my word." He passes his bloody cutlass to someone nearby, who hurriedly wipes it with a rag.

One of the men who had been holding Briggs, whips off his woollen hat and presses it to the bleeding stump. My gaze roams across the the crate and settles on his severed hand lying on the deck. I don't know how I'm still standing. Then I remember Elias beside me, steady as a rock. He must have seen this sort of thing before. He doesn't so much as flinch.

Jim walks in a circle around a whimpering Briggs and the men supporting his weight. The captain surveys his crew.

"Raise a hand if you have a sister." Hands tentatively lift above a fair few heads. "A sweetheart?" More hands. "A daughter?" More hands. The captain stops before one man near to me. He nods.

"How old is Lizzy now, Smithy?"

"Fifteen, Cap'n."

"Fifteen," Jim clucks his tongue and his gaze darts to me. "The same age Hester was when she started working in taverns. When did you last see your daughter?"

"Half a year ago."

"Does she have a womanly shape now? Pretty young thing? Catching the eyes of boys?"

Smithy turns red and clutches his hat in sweating palms. "I suppose."

Jim turns back to his men and raises his voice. "And if one of these men tried to defile her, what would you do?" He turns back to Smithy.

"I'd cut off more than his hand, Cap'n." Smithy lifts his chin defiantly.

A chorus of laughter and "Aye"s rings out.

"Next time one of you is faced with the choice of whether or not to force yourself onto a woman, I want you to think about what Smithy just said. I want you to think about your sisters, sweethearts and daughters. Hell, every one of you came from a mother. Think about your mother! Think about what you'd do to any man who threatened her. Then make a better choice. Treat the woman in question with respect and maybe, just maybe, you'll leave her loving you instead of loathing you."

He marches towards me, his eyes blazing as his men erupt in conversation.

"Oh," he says, stopping beside Briggs' hand. "Someone feed that to the sharks, and Smithy," he faces the bald and red-faced man. "You're my new First Mate. Congratulations."

"Thank you, Cap'n!" Smithy immediately gets to work dispersing the men and cleaning the deck.

Jim scoops me out of Elias's grasp and into his strong arms. He softly kisses my lips and I kiss him back.

Elias clears his throat and we part, both turning to him. Heat rises in my cheeks and I press my lips together.

"Thank you, old friend," Jim says, nodding to Elias.

"Good to see you haven't lost your touch," Elias says gruffly. "I'll find myself a bunk and leave you two love birds to it." He winks at me and turns away.

Jim leads me into his quarters, through the study and into the bedroom, closing the door softly behind us.

"Are you all right?" he asks, his voice tender.

I nod. No words come. He wipes the tears from my cheeks with his thumbs. His fingers linger on my left cheek, which still throbs. He kisses the tender skin.

"Do you want to be left alone? I'd understand if you didn't want any man touching you."

"No," I croak. "I want you." I cling to his sweat-soaked shirt and press myself against his chest. He holds me gently and kisses the top of my head.

"What can I do?"

"Erm, I could really do with brushing my hair?" I look up at him and a nervous laugh escapes my lips. The corner of his mouth twitches. But, without a word, he leads me to the bed and sits me on the edge of it. He kicks off his boots and crawls behind me on the bed. He sits up on his high knees and ever so gently, begins to comb his fingers through my matted hair. Between the storm and the fight and the incident this evening, my hair is a tangled mess.

Silently and calmly, Jim untangles my locks. I sit there, feeling the warmth of him so close. His presence is comforting and the shakes ease off.

"You may have completely changed every crewman's future with that speech," I say softly.

He grunts in reply.

"No, really."

"I'd like to think so, but some of them will have forgotten by morning."

"I don't think so," I say, trying not to shake my head. "You're very compelling."

"Really?" He sounds surprised.

"They respect you. They trust you. They do what you say. Most of the time." I try not to think about Briggs. "You put it to them in terms they can understand. You may have saved a lot of women some awful nights on their backs. So thank you."

"I hate it, what men to do women." His voice is low and his

breath moves my hair.

I chew the inside of my cheek. His record wasn't squeaky clean. But I didn't want to seem ungrateful. I couldn't let it go, though.

"Briggs said you go whoring in every port."

"Briggs is all mouth." He heaves a sigh and his fingers stop working through my hair. "But he's not entirely wrong. I have sought the company of women and paid for it. I've never forced a woman though. I wouldn't do that."

"You told me it had been a year since you'd laid with a woman."

"No," he corrected cautiously, resuming work on my hair. "I told you it had been a year since I'd been inside a woman. That's different."

"How?" I said with a snort, half turning my head to face him.

"Well, you know, when a woman can't—accommodate me—I please her in other ways."

"Oh." I flush with heat, not just in my cheeks. "That makes sense."

He places his hands on my shoulders and leans close to my ear to whisper, "Shall I show you?"

CHAPTER THIRTEEN

I nod my head slowly. He moves back from me and climbs off the bed, coming to face me. He takes my hands and helps me to stand. He stares into my eyes and unbuttons my dress. His movements are slow and deliberate. He slips my dress down and lets it pool at my feet. He turns his attention to the laces of my bodice, his gaze settling on the rise and fall of my full breasts. He lays my bodice at my feet and gently slips my pantelettes down my legs. I stand before him in just my stockings and boots. He drops to one knee and ever so slowly, unfastens my boots, takes them off and sets them aside. He peels one stocking off, then the other.

Even though he's seen me naked plenty, this time feels different. I feel more vulnerable than ever. He stands in front of me and I see how aroused he is. He lifts his shirt over his head and tosses it aside. I reach out to unfasten his breeches, but he steps out of reach and shakes his head.

"Lie down," he says, his voice little more than a throaty rumble. "In the middle of the bed."

I do as he says, shimmying into the middle and lying back. He walks around to the foot of the bed and I lift my head to watch him. He unfastens his breeches and lets them fall. His cock stands to full attention and he takes it in his hand, stroking it gently as he gazes at my body.

He kneels on the bed and nudges my knees apart. I follow his non-verbal commands, nerves rippling through my body. He lowers himself onto his elbows and wraps his hands around my thighs, his face level with my entrance. I realise what he's going to do just a second before his tongue runs between my soft lips and over that sweet spot he likes so much. I gasp as the shock rushes through me. I drop my head back, my neck unable to hold it up to watch everything.

With a murmur of desire, he runs his tongue in a tight circle right around that hard nub of pleasure. Sparks rush down my legs, making them twitch. He holds me firmly in place as he gently eases two fingers inside me. He moves them slowly in and out while his tongue savours the taste of me.

A whimper escapes my parted lips and I find my legs pulling up the bed, my toes curling and dragging the sheets. His fingers respond by making a "come hither" motion inside me, rubbing slowly back and forth over one smooth spot a few inches inside. His tongue begins to move more quickly. Sometimes circling, other times flicking across my hot button.

"Oh god," I groan. My back arches and I clutch the sheet in my fists.

He holds me still with his free hand and continues to work on me. My pleasure mounts swiftly and I toss my head from side to side. I writhe under his ministrations and my breathing becomes ragged.

Quicker and quicker he probes with his fingers and lashes with his tongue. So much pressure. It courses through every fibre of my body. I thrash wildly but can't escape his firm grip.

"Fuck!" I cry out at the top of my lungs. My legs jut out,

going completely rigid. Another cry bursts from me as a hint of fear rushes through my mind. I have no idea what's happening but I feel a bit like I need to pee. He presses on, ignoring the thrashing of my body.

Warm liquid gushes from inside me and I'm mortified.

"Sorry. Oh God!" I cover my face with my hands.

A throaty chuckle brushes over my slick folds and he slowly pulls his fingers out of me. The fluid doesn't smell and is too oily to be what I think it is. I lift my head, frowning.

"We just found the buried treasure," he says, grinning. I've never seen him smile like that.

"Wh-what?"

"I don't have a name for it, only a technique to make it happen. It's the ultimate climax for a woman. Are you enjoying it?"

"Yes?" I'm so confused.

He moves up the bed on his knees and my gaze locks on to the ten inches of hard muscle staring at me.

"May I fuck your mouth?" His voice is that deep rumble that I feel down in my core and I nod mutely. He kneels beside my head and I turn to face him, opening my mouth wide. He eases into me and his hand reaches down my body, his fingers rubbing gently over the spot he was licking.

I moan as I take him right into my mouth. My eyes close and my chest lifts.

His fingers circle and flick, slowly, matching the long, languid thrusts of his hips. He doesn't push too deep down my throat. I lift a hand to grasp the shaft as my tongue works the head, circling it the way his fingers are circling me.

We mirror each other like that for a long time. He keeps it slow but deeply intense. When I open my eyes and look up his muscled body, his head is tipped back and his mouth hangs open;

a low moan on his breath.

"Oh dear God," he whispers to the ceiling. He returns his gaze to me and looks into my eyes. We hold each other's gaze as he picks up the pace with both his hips and fingers.

I whimper as he thrusts deeper. Each thrust comes with a grunt now. My hand tightens on his cock and I suck the tip as hard as I can.

The sensations rushing up from my opening are otherworldly. His fingers rub frantically over the hard bud and I try to cry out. My full mouth prevents much sound escaping. Tension floods my body and my legs lock in place again. My hips buck wildly.

I'm flying towards the edge of a cliff. I see it in my minds eye and there is nothing I can do to stop myself. More huge cries try to burst from my body but are muffled by his cock. He thrusts harder and deeper, grunting each time his head bumps the back of my throat. My whole body reacts aggressively to the sensation. I careen off the cliff and begin to fall... endlessly. My back arches and my head tears away from his groin. His cock slithers out of me, covered in saliva.

"FUCK!" I scream to the ceiling. His fingers are utterly relentless and my body convulses uncontrollably.

He stops abruptly and moves quickly down the bed, dropping between my rigid legs. He thrusts his cock into me, catching me by surprise. I can't breathe. I'm still flying towards the rocks below. He grabs my knees and presses them up to my chest as he thrusts hungrily into my passage.

I can't see. Nothing but black spots. I'm flying, not falling. I'm exploding and reforming over and over again. Coming harder and harder. I can't scream. I can't breathe.

Jim pants roughly over me, his firm hands pressing down hard on my folded knees.

"Fuck," he moans. "You're incredible. Come again, Hester."

I can't obey. I'm powerless. Lost to this feeling of dying and living and coming.

Breath rushes into my lungs and the biggest cry of all bursts from my mouth.

His cock swells inside me and his hips thrust harder, slamming into me again and again as he pumps me full of his seed with heavy groans.

He keeps going and I don't believe he'll ever stop. He's going to fuck me until we both die. Gush after gush of his seed and whatever golden elixir he's managed to make me produce flow from us both.

Finally, his hips slow to long, gentle thrusts as he milks every last drop from his cock. He releases my knees and they flop limply onto the bed. My vision begins to return and my gaze settles on his face.

He pulls out of me and rocks back on his knees. His skin shines with sweat and his breathing is laboured.

I try to speak but only a croak comes out. I try again with more luck.

"Damn," I manage.

"What?" He looks at me with concern in his tired eyes.

"I wanted you to come in my mouth."

"Why?" He frowns.

"With how much rum you drank earlier, I thought it might taste of coconut."

He bursts into the biggest belly laugh I've ever heard and an exhausted smile spreads across my face. I did it. I made him laugh.

We spend the whole night sleeping and fucking; then sleeping and fucking some more. It's a blur of desire and torment in the darkness. Torment because I know it's our last night together and there are words I cannot bring myself to say. If he feels the way I do, he's not letting on either. A shadow hangs over every touch, every climax.

When dawn peeks over the horizon, he's gently spooning me. Both of us half asleep but unable to stop ourselves from coupling. It's as if it's a primal need in both of us. Desperately clinging to the life raft of his bed.

One of his hands softly cups one of my breasts and the other rests on my hip, holding it still while he rocks slowly in and out of me.

"Daylight," I croak, my voice hoarse from so much panting and screaming through the night.

"Hmm," he replies, his breath on my ear. "I don't care. Fuck the gold. I want to stay here with you forever."

My heart skips a beat.

The clang of the ship's bell destroys our fragile utopia.

"Land, ho!" A shout calls from above us. Jim groans and pulls out of me. I flop onto my back as he rolls away. He's already off the bed and pulling his trousers on. Years of practice at responding quickly to his crew take over his yearning for me and I can't be jealous. I actually admire him for it.

"Get dressed if you want to come ashore with us," he says softly. He pulls his shirt on and leans over the bed to kiss me tenderly.

"Is it safe?"

"It should be. We left Kane and the Sea Devil in tatters. They shouldn't have been able to follow us." He moves towards the door, his boots in one hand. He glances back at me for one last look of longing before leaving the room.

I rub my face and let out a throaty groan. Exhaustion clings to every muscle but I am curious to see what we find.

I crawl from the bed and wash myself at the basin. I pick up my clothes, remembering that my dress is torn. All of my other clothes are in my bag under my bunk, at the other end of the ship. I dress in Jim's clothes, tucking the oversized shirt into the breeches and fastening a belt as tight as it'll go. I make my way out into the sunlight, shielding my eyes from the bright sun blazing over the horizon. Jim stands up on the quarterdeck at the helm with Elias and the helmsman. I watch them for a minute, their attention is firmly on the sea ahead. I walk to the starboard side and lean out over the rail. A string of islands dots the sea ahead like pearls. I turn and climb the stairs up to the quarterdeck, my calf muscles burning with the effort.

"Morning, Miss," Elias says with a wry smile.

"Morning." I move towards them and Jim finally looks at me. A wide smile crosses his face and he scoops me up in his arms. He turns me to look at the islands and points. I follow his finger, not really caring what he wants me to see, I just love being held by him.

"There," he whispers in my ear. "That one."

"Aye," Elias says beside us. "And best be quick about it."

Jim releases me and steps aside. "Out with the studding sails!"

The call is met with an immediate flurry of movement. Crewmen spring into action, scrambling up the shrouds and onto the yards, their hands deft as they unfurl the extra sails. The long booms are swung outward, extending beyond the main rigging, and within moments, pale canvas billows out, catching the warm wind that sweeps in from the sea.

"Brace those yards!" Jim barks, his voice carrying over the deck.

The men haul on the lines, tightening the sheets and adjusting the angles to make full use of the breeze. The ship lurches slightly as the fresh wind fills the additional sails, and I feel the subtle shift beneath my feet as The Stormchaser picks up speed, cutting through the waves with newfound urgency.

Elias watches the men work with an approving nod, though his fingers tap absently against the hilt of his belt knife. “Should get us there before midday,” he says.

Jim glances at him. “If the wind holds.”

I turn my gaze to the island in the distance. It looks peaceful from here, a slip of green rising from the endless blue. But if this is where the Spanish gold is hidden, then there’s no telling what dangers await us on its shores.

Jim must be thinking the same thing because he calls over his shoulder, “Have the men arm themselves. No one sets foot on that island unprepared.”

A ripple of acknowledgement spreads through the deck as muskets are checked and blades fastened to belts. Whatever awaits us beyond the shallows, we won’t be walking into it blindly.

CHAPTER FOURTEEN

The sea is a glassy blue, the morning sun casting golden streaks across the gentle waves. The islands rise ahead of us, dark green against the bright sky, their thick foliage forming an unbroken canopy at their centres. Elias stands beside Jim near the helm, his sharp eyes fixed on the land ahead, his fingers twitching as he points toward the longest of the islands.

“That one,” he says. "The map’s markings match the shape of its coast. There’s a narrow inlet just beyond that rise.” He gestures toward a break in the tree line where the land slopes gently toward the water. “We anchor here and row in. The reef surrounding it is too shallow for the ship.”

Jim nods. “Smithy, prepare to drop anchor.”

“Aye, Captain!” The new First Mate, a stocky, weathered man with sharp eyes and a steady hand, moves swiftly across the deck, barking orders to the crew. The air hums with activity as ropes are secured, sails are furled, and the anchor chain rattles as it plunges into the deep. The Stormchaser slows, then stills, rocking gently with the tide.

I grip the rail, peering at the shoreline ahead. The island looks untouched and wild, a place few men have likely set foot.

My pulse quickens at the thought. The treasure is buried beneath thick jungle, hidden away, waiting to be claimed.

The crew readies the longboats, lowering them into the water with practised ease. Oars clatter, crates of supplies are loaded, and Jim strides toward the railing, his expression set with determination. Elias follows close behind, moving slower, his injuries still hampering him, but there is a hunger in his eyes that mirrors my own.

"I'm coming with you," I say before Jim can even speak.

He pauses, glancing at me, then at the island. "Hester—"

"You'll need another set of hands," I argue, squaring my shoulders. "I won't slow you down."

He exhales through his nose but doesn't argue. Instead, he jerks his head toward the longboat. "Get in."

I barely contain my excitement as I climb down the ladder and settle into one of the small boats, gripping the sides as the oarsmen take their positions. Jim follows, dropping down beside me, while Elias takes the seat near the bow.

"Smithy, you're in charge till we return," Jim calls up to the deck.

"Aye, Captain," Smithy replies, watching us closely as we push off from the ship.

The longboats cut through the water, the rhythm of the oars steady and sure. The scent of salt lingers in the air, mixing with the humid, earthy smell wafting from the island. As we draw closer, the trees seem to loom taller, the shadows beneath their branches dark and impenetrable.

Treasure or not, something about this place feels different.

I tighten my grip on the boat's edge, heart pounding with anticipation as the bow of the longboat scrapes against the sand.

The moment we hit the shore, the crew jumps out, boots sinking into the damp, golden sand. Jim steps down beside me, scanning the tree line while the others pull the boats further up the beach. The jungle ahead is thick but not impenetrable, its humid air carrying the scent of wet earth and unseen flowers. Elias wastes no time, adjusting his belt and nodding toward the path ahead.

"This way," he grunts, already moving into the undergrowth. "It's not far."

We follow, hacking through ferns and thick vines as the jungle swallows us whole. Though the island is small, the canopy overhead makes it feel vast, the dappled sunlight barely penetrating the thick foliage. The air is alive with the chirps of unseen birds and the occasional rustle of movement in the underbrush, but Elias moves with certainty, his steps confident. He's been here before.

"I buried it just beyond these trees," he says, glancing back over his shoulder. "Left it wrapped up well."

Jim and I exchange a look. If the gold is still here, this will be the end of our search.

Minutes later, Elias stops, pushing aside a cluster of thick fronds. Before us lies a patch of disturbed earth, different from the rest of the jungle floor. He kneels, brushing his fingers over the soil, then nods. "Here. Help me dig."

The crew needs no further encouragement. Using their hands, cutlasses, and whatever tools they brought, they dig into the damp earth, the rich scent of soil rising into the air. It doesn't take long. Soon, the tip of a canvas-wrapped bundle emerges, then another. Excited hands pull at the coverings, revealing gleaming bricks of Spanish gold beneath.

"Hell's teeth," one of the men mutters in awe. "That's a fortune."

Elias grins, clapping the nearest sailor on the back. "Aye. And now it's ours."

One by one, we haul the bundles from their shallow grave, stacking them onto cloth tarps to be carried. The weight of it is staggering, but adrenaline and victory keep us moving. The men work with renewed vigour, sweat gleaming on their foreheads as they lift the treasure and begin the slow trek back to the longboats.

Jim watches, arms crossed, his expression unreadable. I step beside him, my own heart still racing.

"It's over, then?" I ask quietly.

He glances at me, a small smirk playing at the corner of his lips. "Almost. Let's get it back to the ship first."

And with that, we follow the crew, carrying our fortune toward the waiting boats.

The first load of gold is nearly aboard when a shout comes from one of the men standing watch near the water's edge. "Sails! North of the island!"

Every head snaps up. I spin, shielding my eyes against the glare of the sun. A ship looms on the horizon, her torn sails a ragged silhouette against the bright sky. Even from this distance, I recognize the damaged hulk. The Sea Devil has found us.

"Move!" Jim bellows, his voice slicing through the stunned silence. "Get that gold aboard, now!"

The crew erupts into motion, muscles straining as they haul the last of the treasure toward the waiting longboats. Oars splash into the water, men pushing off before their boots are even fully planted. The urgency in the air is thick, crackling with the unspoken knowledge that Kane will not come for parley. He'll come for blood.

Elias grimaces, his grip tight on his bundle as he steps into the nearest boat. "Knew we hadn't seen the last of that bastard."

Jim shoves another bundle of gold into a waiting sailor's arms before turning to me. "Get in. Now."

I don't argue. I climb into the last longboat, heart hammering as the crew rows with everything they have, the island shrinking behind us as we cut through the waves toward The Stormchaser. Every stroke is a battle against time. Behind us, the Sea Devil creeps closer, a dark predator on the hunt.

"They're still fixing their rigging," Elias mutters, his keen eyes locked on the enemy vessel. "They won't be at full speed, but they'll still catch us if we waste time."

Jim's jaw tightens as we near the side of The Stormchaser. "Smithy! Prepare to make sail! We're leaving now!"

A chorus of "Aye, Cap'n!" rises from the deck as we pull alongside. Hands reach down to haul the gold aboard, then us. I scramble up, my boots hitting the deck just as Jim swings over the railing behind me.

"All hands to stations! Haul up the anchor! Get those sails full!" Jim's voice is a whipcrack of command, and the deck explodes into a frenzy of movement. Ropes are thrown, pulleys creak, and the anchor groans as it is lifted from the depths. The ship lurches, the wind catching the sails as the helmsman pulls her around.

The Sea Devil is still bearing down on us, but we have the advantage of readiness. The sails snap taut, and The Stormchaser leaps forward, cutting through the sea like a blade.

Jim steps to the helm, his face set in determination. "We make for Nassau. Kane won't follow us into a fleet of privateers."

The deck hums with tense energy as we gain speed, the wind filling every stitch of canvas. I grip the railing, my breath unsteady. We have the gold. Now, we just need to keep it.

Jim barks orders with the sharp precision of a man who knows every second counts. "Brace the yards! Keep those sails drawing full! We need every knot we can get!"

The crew scrambles, tightening ropes and adjusting the

sails to catch every breath of wind. The Stormchaser leaps forward, her sleek hull cutting through the waves, but the Sea Devil is relentless. Though her sails are patched and her rigging not at full strength, she still gives chase, her bow splitting the water as she closes the gap.

"They're coming on fast!" one of the men shouts from the rigging.

Jim curses under his breath before turning to Smithy. "Out with the studding sails! We need to push her harder!"

At once, the crew rushes to deploy the extra canvas, unfurling the studding sails beyond the main rigging. The wind catches them, and The Stormchaser surges forward, her speed increasing with every heartbeat.

I steal a glance behind us. The Sea Devil is still there, but the distance is growing. Slowly, foot by foot, we're pulling away.

"Come on, girl," Elias mutters under his breath, watching the sails billow overhead. "Give us all you've got."

The wind holds steady, pushing us along as the island fades into the distance. The tension lingers, every man watching the Sea Devil, waiting, wondering if she will find some hidden reserve of speed and close the gap again. But as the minutes drag on, it becomes clear—we're winning.

"They're falling behind!" someone shouts, and a ragged cheer rises from the crew.

Jim exhales, his grip on the helm easing just slightly. "We keep our heading. Full speed until we reach Nassau. No one lets up until we drop anchor in safe waters."

The men nod, but the weight of relief is already creeping in. The Sea Devil may still be there, lurking, but for now, she's nothing more than a shadow on the horizon.

I glance at Jim, the tension still evident in his jaw. His knuckles are white where he grips the wheel, his gaze locked on the horizon. If the weather holds, we'll make Nassau before the Sea Devil can catch us.

The tension on the deck eases by degrees as the chase settles into a distant threat rather than an immediate danger. The men move with purpose, but the frantic energy of flight fades, leaving only the rhythmic hum of the wind in the sails and the steady creak of the timbers beneath our feet.

I slip away from the rail, the salt air still tingling against my skin as I move toward the lower deck. My thoughts whirl, not of the gold, not of the chase, but of the man standing at the helm. Jim Blackthorne, the man who keeps his past locked away like a chest with no key.

Elias is exactly where I expect him to be, sitting on a barrel near the galley, rubbing a hand over his weathered face. He glances up as I approach, a knowing glint in his tired eyes.

"Ah, I was wonderin' when you'd come sniffing for answers," he mutters, shifting slightly to make room for me to sit.

I lower myself onto a crate opposite him, folding my hands in my lap. "I know little more than scraps," I admit. "But I know there's something dark in his past. Something about his father. Something... unforgivable. He's a good man, brought up well. How did he come to be a pirate?"

Elias exhales through his nose, shaking his head. "Aye. It's a story, that's for certain. A cruel one." He looks me over, measuring something in my gaze before nodding. "If anyone should know it, it ought to be you."

I don't interrupt. I don't push him. I let him tell it in his own time.

"Jim had a wife once," Elias begins. "A good woman, sharp as a blade and twice as dangerous when she needed to be. A smuggler, before she met him. His father hated her for it—thought she was beneath him, unfit for the family name." He pauses, rubbing at his temple as if the memory itself pains him. "But Jim loved her. Married her anyway. They had a little girl, barely walking when it all went to hell."

My breath catches in my throat, but I say nothing.

Elias continues, voice quieter now. "His father was determined to break them apart. Couldn't have a son of his mixed up with smugglers. So he had her framed—claimed she was still running goods, that she was using Jim to move her wares. Jim stood by her, of course. Wouldn't be turned against her, not by lies, not by threats. So the old man made sure she wouldn't be a problem any more."

A chill runs through me. "What did he do?"

Elias' jaw tightens. "Had her killed. The babe too. Called it an accident, a tragic loss at sea." He shakes his head. "But Jim knew better. Knew exactly who was behind it. That's when he turned his back on the Blackthorne business. Stole his father's ship and took to the sea for good."

I swallow hard, my heart aching for the man standing above deck, staring into the horizon as if he could outrun the ghosts of his past.

"He says he owes you his life. It's why he risked so much to rescue you. I don't think he cares one bit about the gold."

Elias chuckles and rubs his hands across his stubble again. "Aye. Sounds like our boy. I don't know about owing me his life, but I helped him get away. I made sure he had the deeds to this ship and the paperwork to cut ties from his father's business. I helped him get away clear without a warrant for his arrest."

"Why didn't you go with him?"

"Because I'm too old for this life now, lass. I was thinkin' about retiring. So I stayed put. But Blackthorne Senior found out my role and I was dismissed from the company anyway. Been trying to make ends meet for three years now and hoping I'd find

Jim. But he found me." A smile tugs at his whiskers.

"You're a good friend. I can see why he values you."

"That's kind, lass. Be careful with that good heart of yours. Jim won't love again," Elias murmurs. "Not properly. Not unless someone's willing to break through all that wreckage." He looks at me then, his gaze sharp, searching. "So the question is, lass—are you willing?"

I stare down at my hands, Elias's words settling deep into my bones. The weight of Jim's past, the pain he carries, is more than I ever imagined. But it doesn't scare me away. If anything, it makes me want to hold on tighter. To show him that not all love is doomed to be lost at sea.

CHAPTER FIFTEEN

The Stormchaser glides into Nassau's bustling harbour, her sails catching the fading light, turning the canvas a warm amber hue. The evening air carries the scent of salt, tar, and distant spices from the markets beyond the docks. Ahead, the city sprawls across the coastline, its wooden buildings clustered in haphazard rows, their windows glowing like fireflies against the twilight. The sounds of Nassau rise to greet us—laughter, shouting, the creak of ships settling into their berths, and the occasional raucous tune from a waterfront tavern spilling out into the humid air.

Jim stands at the helm, his posture relaxed but his grip firm, guiding the ship with the effortless ease of a man who has spent more years at sea than on land. The wind ruffles his dark hair, but his expression remains unreadable, his gaze sharp and calculating as he navigates through the tangle of anchored vessels. The Stormchaser responds to his touch like a well-trained beast, and for a moment, I simply watch him, taking in the quiet authority he carries, the way the crew instinctively follows his lead without question. I stand beside him, my heart heavier than I expected. The ship slows, the anchor drops, and the crew moves with swift precision, tying her off against the dock.

My time aboard is ending.

Jim turns to me, his expression measured, though something unreadable lingers in his eyes. He reaches into his coat with slow deliberation, withdrawing a bulging, leather pouch. He weighs it in his palm for a moment before offering it to me.

"As promised," he says, his voice low and thick with emotion.

When I take it, the leather is warm from his body, and the weight of it makes my breath hitch. Thirty guineas. More money than I have ever held in my life, let alone called my own. It's enough to change everything. Enough to start over.

I untie the leather cord and let the pouch gape open, revealing the glint of gold within. The coins are smooth beneath my fingertips, their edges worn from years of trade and travel. They seem almost too bright in the dimming light, each one a small promise of freedom, of choices I never dared to consider before. My fingers tighten around the pouch, a mixture of gratitude and unease warring within me. More wealth than I've ever had. More than I know what to do with. I swallow hard and tighten my grip around the purse, nodding.

"Thank you."

He hesitates, but before he can say anything more, I turn away. My fingers brush against the coin in my pocket—the one I took from Briggs back at the tavern. My steps carry me below deck, the familiar scent of salt, rum, and sweat thick in the galley. There, sitting alone at a table, is Briggs. He nurses a cup of rum in his remaining hand. The other wrist is well wrapped in bandages.

I don't hesitate. I slide the gold coin across the table to him.

"I want nothing from you."

Briggs looks at the coin, then at me. There's something in his eyes I can't place, but I don't wait to decipher it. I turn on my heel and leave.

Back on deck, Jim stands near the gangplank, arms folded across his chest, his gaze fixed on the docks. The lanterns lining the waterfront sway gently in the evening breeze, their glow casting long shadows across the worn planks. The town is alive, pulsing with activity—merchants tallying their wares, sailors unloading barrels, drunken voices rising from the nearest alehouse. It's chaos, but to a man like Jim, I imagine it's simply another part of the world he calls home. I hesitate, watching him from a few steps away, feeling the weight of unspoken words between us. The air is alive with the sounds of Nassau—traders calling out their wares, drunken sailors laughing, the occasional clash of steel from a street brawl already underway.

Jim turns towards me, his broad shoulders set with a tension I can't quite name. There's a stiffness to his stride, a hesitance as if he, too, feels the enormity of this moment. The world outside The Stormchaser is loud and demanding, full of choices that weren't there when I was just a girl serving drinks in a tavern. I glance up at him, searching for something in his face, but his gaze is already scanning the crowd, ever the wary captain. "I'll help you find a ship to take you back to Charleston."

I should be grateful, but the thought of leaving twists something deep inside me. I glance at him, forcing the words out. "I don't want to go back. There's nothing for me there."

Jim looks at me, searching. "Then what will you do?"

I inhale deeply, the scent of sea spray and distant woodsmoke grounding me, though the weight of the gold in my pocket feels heavier than it should. The thought of using it to secure a home of my own, to carve out a place in this unpredictable world, is both thrilling and terrifying. My voice is steady when I finally speak. "I might buy a house. Somewhere here in the Bahamas. A place where the sea is always close, but the ground is steady beneath my feet."

His expression flickers—something unreadable, guarded. "Aye?"

I nod, my throat tight. "You could visit, whenever you're in the area."

He exhales sharply, looking away. "Hester—"

But I don't let him finish. I place a hand lightly on his forearm, stopping him. "Elias told me everything," I say softly, watching the way his jaw tightens. "About your wife. Your daughter. Your father. I know now why you carry so much on your shoulders, why you hold yourself apart from the world." The words hang between us, heavy as lead, and for a moment, I think he might turn away. But he doesn't.

Jim stills, his entire body rigid. When his eyes meet mine again, there's a storm there, raw and unguarded. "Did he, now?"

"He did. And I understand now. I know why you push people away. But Jim—" I step closer, barely a breath between us. "I love you."

For a moment, the silence stretches between us, thick and unyielding. Then I see it—the crack in the carefully built walls around him. It starts in his eyes, a flicker of raw emotion, something breaking loose from where it's been buried deep. Before I can say another word, he closes the space between us, his hands coming to cradle my face, his touch warm, almost reverent. And then he kisses me—fiercely, desperately, as if he's been holding this back for far too long.

When he pulls away, his forehead rests against mine. "Stay with me."

The docks, the world, everything else fades away. "Yes," I

whisper. "Yes."

As the last golden sliver of sunlight disappears over the horizon, his lips find mine once more, softer this time, full of quiet promise. The sounds of Nassau fade into the background, the world narrowing to just the two of us. Whatever the future holds, whatever storms we may still face, I know one thing for certain—I have found my place, and it is here, with him.

THE BOOKBINDER'S FAREWELL

So. You followed her through storms and secrets. Through rope-burned wrists and whispered promises. And still... you stayed.

That tells me something, darling.

You like a man who takes control.

But more than that—you crave a love that cuts, that brands, that binds.

There are more stories waiting for you. More obsessions to feed. More desires to unfurl.

The sea may have claimed her, but the next tale might just claim you.

Until then... *I'll be watching.*

THE HEAT DOESN'T HAVE TO END HERE

Want a glimpse of what happens after the waves settle?

Sign up to my newsletter for exclusive bonus content—including epilogues you won't find anywhere else.
It's free, filthy, and just a little bit forbidden.

Download it here: https://BookHip.com/VTHLHRH

See you between the pages, gorgeous.
Lacey xox

Printed in Dunstable, United Kingdom

67052582R00078